UNDERSTANDING LONGITUDINAL DATA

UNDERSTANDING LONGITUDINAL DATA

EMILY GILBERT

Sage

Sage

1 Oliver's Yard
55 City Road
London EC1Y 1SP

2455 Teller Road
Thousand Oaks
California 91320

Unit No 323-333, Third Floor, F-Block
International Trade Tower
Nehru Place, New Delhi - 110 019

8 Marina View Suite 43-053
Asia Square Tower 1
Singapore 018960

Editor: Charlotte Bush
Editorial assistant: Rhiannon Holt
Production editor: Victoria Nicholas
Copyeditor: Diana Chambers
Proofreader: Clare Weaver
Indexer: Martin Hargreaves
Marketing manager: Ben Sherwood
Cover design: Shaun Mercier
Typeset by: C&M Digitals (P) Ltd, Chennai, India
Printed in the UK

Library of Congress Control Number: 2023933351

British Library Cataloguing in Publication data

A catalogue record for this book is available from the British Library

ISBN 978-1-5297-2724-1
ISBN 978-1-5297-2723-4 (pbk)

Contents

Author Biography

Emily Gilbert is a Principal Research Officer at the London Mayor's Office for Policing And Crime. She designs and manages surveys of residents and victims of crime, focused on attitudes towards, and experiences of, policing in London. She obtained an MA in Longitudinal Social Research, followed by a PhD in Survey Methodology from the Institute for Social and Economic Research at the University of Essex, writing her thesis on the sources of measurement error in panel surveys. She has previously worked as a Survey Manager at the Centre for Longitudinal Studies, University College London, on the design and implementation of the British birth cohort studies housed there. Her research interests centre on issues around attitude measurement, data quality, longitudinal data collection, and the use of new technology and innovative methods for data collection.

Preface

Longitudinal studies have always fascinated me, right from when I first heard the term, aged 17, when I was studying for my A-levels. This fascination went on to shape my further study and ultimately my career. The rich insight that longitudinal studies across the world are able to offer is arguably unparalleled, cutting across a range of disciplines and research areas. This has led to an abundance of longitudinal datasets available for secondary analysis, offering infinite research possibilities.

There seems to be an overwhelming number of books describing in detail the analytical methods appropriate for longitudinal data analysis, all of which are valuable. However, what I found was missing in my early years of working with longitudinal data was a resource that took a step back from that and addressed more fundamental issues around the use of longitudinal data – what is interesting about longitudinal data, how it can be utilised effectively, and what you need to understand about the features of both the data and the study design before you undertake analysis. It is my hope that this book answers these questions serving as a handbook that outlines the opportunities and challenges of using longitudinal data for students and practitioners alike.

I have many people to thank for the existence of this book, from my first sociology teacher who sparked my interest in longitudinal studies, through to the many fabulous academics at the University of Essex who nurtured and encouraged this interest to develop into a passion. The wonderful team at Sage who have helped me turn the seed of an idea into a reality. Finally, my family and friends, who have provided constant encouragement and support to get this book finished.

1

WHAT IS LONGITUDINAL RESEARCH?

OVERVIEW OF CONTENT

This chapter will provide you with the fundamental and basic information about longitudinal studies. It will answer the key question, 'What is a longitudinal study?' and then explain the advantages and disadvantages of using a longitudinal methodology to conduct research.

Some of the advantages and disadvantages introduced in this chapter will be expanded on further in separate chapters in this book, and this is signposted where necessary.

As well as a practical explanation of longitudinal studies, the chapter will also provide a short introduction to one of the major theoretical issues associated with longitudinal studies – developing a theory of change.

Learning outcomes

After you have read this chapter, you will be able to:

- understand what a longitudinal study is;
- describe the benefits of carrying out research using a longitudinal methodology;
- describe the drawbacks of longitudinal studies;
- understand what a theory of change is.

WHAT IS A LONGITUDINAL STUDY?

At its most basic, a **longitudinal study** is one that follows the same subjects over time, taking repeated measures from them. By taking repeated measurements over time, a longitudinal study is a method by which to study change. Longitudinal studies can last weeks, months or even years. By following the same subjects for so long, researchers can see how different things change or stay the same over time, such as attitudes, behaviours, health conditions, educational or career paths, or relationships and family structure. This stability or change can also be looked at in relation to past events or experiences, establishing how certain events and experiences can impact on various outcomes.

The subjects followed by longitudinal studies are called '**sampling units**'. Sampling units are the single items that make up the population of interest. The **population** is the entire cohort of interest. For instance, this could be all the people who attend a certain school, the entire population of a city or country, or all the businesses in a certain sector. Sampling units are chosen to represent the population and can be individuals, households or businesses, for example. These are the entities that are followed over time.

In longitudinal studies with a social or medical focus, sampling units are most often people or households, allowing researchers to see how people's situations, behaviours, attitudes and lives change over time. By looking at these changes in relation to people's experiences in life, and the circumstances in which they grow up and live, we can understand how people's pasts can shape their future.

Each time that a longitudinal study conducts a follow-up survey, it is usually referred to as a '**wave**' or a '**sweep**', with the first survey being the baseline wave or wave 1. Longitudinal studies can (technically) contain just two waves or any number above that. Numerous longitudinal studies around the world have been running for many years, with multiple waves of data collection having taken place.

Longitudinal studies are generally **observational**, meaning that researchers observe what is happening but do not influence or manipulate events. Observational data can be collected using interviews or questionnaires, or by the researcher watching and noting situations or behaviours. A more recent development involves using administrative data to follow people over time. Rather than talking directly to the people involved in the longitudinal study, administrative information such as health records, education records and financial records are accessed on a regular basis in order to build up a picture of change over time for individuals. The observational approach is in contrast to the use of **experimental data**, where researchers control which participants are exposed to different events or situations in order to see how outcomes vary.

Longitudinal studies are used in a variety of fields across the social sciences to explore a multitude of events and outcomes.

- Sociology: examining life events, choices and circumstances over time to study the impacts of these events, choices and circumstances on a range of outcomes, including sociodemographic, well-being, and so on.

- Psychology: understanding changes in thoughts, emotions and behaviours and the impact this has on mental health and well-being.
- Economics: looking at changes in socioeconomic characteristics, behaviours and decisions to understand economic resources across time.
- Population health: measuring how health-related behaviours and attitudes affect health-based outcomes.

As has been alluded to, longitudinal studies follow people over time. This requires collecting data about an individual more than once at different points in time. In an ideal world, data for a longitudinal study should be collected at three time points at a minimum, but generally the more the better (Chan, 1998). While many studies have a two time-point design, this does not allow us to see intra-individual change across time; by default, any change is linear, which is unlikely to adequately or accurately describe what is really happening. In addition, true change may be confounded with **measurement error** in a two-wave design (Singer and Willett, 2003). As such, three waves or more are preferable.

WHAT DOES LONGITUDINAL DATA OFFER OVER CROSS-SECTIONAL DATA?

In contrast to longitudinal studies, **cross-sectional studies** generally ask the same questions to different people at different points in time. This gives us a 'snapshot' of what is happening at a particular point in time. Cross-sectional studies can also allow us to see how attitudes or behaviours have changed at a population level between the different time-points. However, this approach doesn't allow us to see what is happening on an individual level. It could be that some groups of people have changed in one way and a different group have changed in a different way, but this is lost when looking at the population level.

An example of this is poverty. Cross-sectional data appear to show that a certain proportion of the population are in poverty at different points in time, and the assumption using cross-sectional data was that it was always the same group who were experiencing poverty. However, longitudinal data from the British Household Panel Survey (BHPS; see the study profile of the UK Household Longitudinal Study, which incorporated the BHPS sample, in this chapter) showed that actually on an individual level there was a lot of change in who was experiencing poverty. Some individuals moved into poverty, while others were moving out. While the proportion of the population in poverty remained relatively stable, there were many changes on the individual level (Jarvis and Jenkins, 1996). Why is it important to understand this? If we can understand the circumstances that are causing people to enter or exit poverty, we can create policies more effectively to try to move people out of poverty and keep them out.

Research spotlight

Jarvis, S. and Jenkins, S.P. (1996) 'Changing places: Income mobility and poverty dynamics in Britain'

This paper was one of the first to show mobility in income and poverty on an individual level across a long period of time. Statistics about income and poverty in the UK were usually derived from cross-sectional datasets, which provided an overall picture of income and poverty levels at a given point in time, but were unable to show what was happening at an individual level. Jarvis and Jenkins instead looked at data from the British Household Panel Survey, which followed a large number of households over time, interviewing them annually from 1991 onwards. What they found was striking.

While official figures showed a relatively stable level of income and poverty in the UK at the time, there was a lot of change at the household level. This change was experienced by households all across the income distribution, from the poor to the wealthy. In fact, when you split the income distribution of all households in the BHPS into ten even-sized groups from year to year around 60 per cent of households moved groups. When Jarvis and Jenkins looked at those with the lowest incomes, they found many people moving into this group, as well as many households managing to leave this category.

This finding was only possible with longitudinal data. This insight into income and poverty dynamics in the UK highlighted the need for changes in policy that aimed to target those persistently experiencing poverty. The longitudinal data highlighted the complex and ever-changing nature of poverty for households in the UK, offering greater depth than that found in cross-sectional data.

STUDY **PROFILE**

The UK Household Longitudinal Study (Understanding Society)

Established: 2009 (although it incorporates the sample from its predecessor study, the British Household Panel Study, which began in 1991).

Country: United Kingdom.

Sampling unit: households.

Sample size at base: c. 40,000 households.

Frequency of interviews: annually.

Participants: all adults (16+) resident in the sampled household; 10–15-year-old adolescents, resident in the sampled household.

Topics covered: family life, employment, education, finances, health, well-being.

Methods of data collection: face-to-face interviews or online self-completion questionnaires.

Innovative features: ethnic minority boost,[1] bio-measure collection,[2] data linkage.[3]

Data availability: data are available to the research community via the UK Data Service.

More information: www.understandingsociety.ac.uk

PROS AND CONS OF LONGITUDINAL RESEARCH

As with any research approach, there are both advantages and disadvantages to collecting and using longitudinal data. The next section will outline some of these pros and cons.

Pros: what does longitudinal research offer?

As earlier parts of this chapter have alluded to, there are many advantages of longitudinal data. Many of them centre around the unique nature of longitudinal data and the complex questions it allows us to answer. Here we will explore some of those advantages in more detail.

Understanding how the past shapes the future

As discussed previously, longitudinal research allows us to understand how the past can shape the future. We can see how certain events and experiences may lead to different outcomes in life, and look at sequences of events and their impact on different outcomes. We can also look at the timing and duration of events to see how outcomes differ when these factors vary. For example, thinking again about poverty, an individual who experiences poverty for a number of years may be affected in different ways across the course of their life from someone who is living in poverty for a few months. Alternatively, living in poverty for a year in your twenties may lead to different outcomes compared to living in poverty for a year in your sixties. Only longitudinal data can allow us to explore the impact of the past on the future in a nuanced way.

Human recall advantages

If a prospective design is used, where individuals are recruited and then followed to assess outcomes (see Chapter 2 for more information), they are often not required to report on detailed information from the past. Instead, they often are just required to recall events that have happened since the last interview. If the interviews are relatively frequent, this may not be too much of a burdensome task in terms of memory and recall.

Conversely, if a cross-sectional approach is taken, a respondent may be asked to recall a wealth of information from across an entire life span – for example, recalling significant life events, dates they occurred, changes in employment or income, health events, and so on.

The human memory is not perfect, which can cause biases in the data collected. By visiting participants regularly in the way that a longitudinal study does, problems associated with memory and recall can be reduced, offering benefits over cross-sectional study designs (see Chapter 6 for more information).

Disentangling age, period and cohort effects

Age, **period** and **cohort effects** can be disentangled using some longitudinal studies, depending on the design. **Age effects** are those occurrences that are related to the biological age of an individual. For example, if we think about cognition, changes occur over the life-course. As a person ages biologically, their cognition will change, and this affects most people in a similar way. **Period effects** are those that affect everybody, of any age, at the same time. They are external influences, such as economic depression, civil unrest, and so on. For example, the global financial crisis of 2008 likely affected most people, regardless of how old they were at the time. Cohort effects are occurrences that are unique to a specific group of people based on a common factor between them, and common experiences or occurrences across time. A common type of cohort is that of individuals who are all born in the same year, known as a birth cohort. Their experiences are unique as they age, so their experience at age 50 will be different from a group of people who are born 20 years later at age 50.

Longitudinal studies can help us to understand changes and experiences across different groups in terms of age, period and cohort effects, disentangling the three to understand what is happening for different groups of people over time and how those experiences are unique or similar, depending on age, period or cohort (Blanchard et al., 1977).

Research spotlight

Blanchard, R.D., Bunker, J.B. and Wachs, M. (1977) 'Distinguishing aging, period and cohort effects in longitudinal studies of elderly populations'

Blanchard and colleagues recognised that it is important to disentangle age, period and cohort effects in order to fully understand the diverse experiences of different groups of people. Their paper uses census data from Los Angeles County in the US from 1940, 1950, 1960 and 1970 to look at a multitude of variables related to housing

and living conditions, including single-person households, rates of home ownership and rental, house prices and cost of renting. The authors were particularly interested in the elderly population of Los Angeles and their experiences of these things, so they disentangle age, period and cohort effects from the census data to understand more about this group.

At the time, the authors report that policy-makers tended to view the problems experienced by the elderly as related to the effects of aging. However, examination of the data for age, period and cohort effects showed that the issues were not purely about aging, but also influenced by factors independent of aging. They found that period effects related to technological development, economic circumstances and the housing market. In addition, there were cohort effects, which meant that the particular generation they studied would have unique experiences not experienced by younger generations as they aged.

This practical example shows how the untangling of age, period and cohort effects can be particularly important for understanding the experiences of certain groups of people and was only possible through the use of longitudinal data. It is also a nice example of how longitudinal data can be administrative, rather than collected directly from individuals via questionnaires and interviews.

Natural experiments

Longitudinal studies can take advantage of **natural experiments**. A natural experiment is one where researchers do not manipulate conditions for different research participants in the way that would happen in a more traditional experiment, but rather where in the real world, different people end up in different conditions or circumstances as a result of something external that has happened 'naturally'. For example, during the course of a study, a policy may be implemented unevenly across the sample of study participants simply due to how the implementation has occurred in the real world and not as a result of anything the researcher has done. If the study has participants living under both 'conditions', the study can explore how the conditions impact people differently. An example of this type of natural experiment can be seen with tobacco warning labels. Over the last two decades, health warnings have been increasingly added to the packaging of tobacco products, but this has occurred at different times and in different forms in different countries. The International Tobacco Control Policy Evaluation Project (ITC) is the world's first international **cohort study** focusing on tobacco use. One research project using ITC data looked at adult smokers living in the United States, Canada, Australia and the United Kingdom, to assess how effective the introduction of warning labels on cigarettes had been on knowledge around the risks of smoking (Hammond et al., 2006).

Research spotlight

Hammond, F., McNeill, B. and Cummings, K.M. (2006) 'Effectiveness of cigarette warning labels in informing smokers about the risks of smoking: Findings from the International Tobacco Control (ITC) four country survey'

The International Tobacco Control Four Country Survey (ITC-4) contained a group of respondents from the United States, Canada, UK and Australia, interviewed regularly by telephone. One of the aims of the ITC-4 was to look at the impact of different forms of warnings on cigarette packaging.

In each country, different types of warning, such as text warnings or images, were implemented at different times. This allowed researchers to look at how effective each type of warning was at increasing awareness of the risks of cigarette smoking.

They found that Canada's policy of using graphic images on cigarette packages was more effective in informing smokers about the risks than text warnings used in the other three countries. When the UK implemented larger text warnings on packaging, more UK smokers reported noticing the warnings and feeling deterred from smoking. When Australia introduced graphic image warnings, more respondents noticed the warnings and were more likely not to smoke as a result. This led to the conclusion that larger warnings were likely to be more effective, as were pictorial warnings.

It is not possible to implement a randomised control trial in this situation - researchers can't randomly assign smokers to be exposed to different types of warnings on their cigarette packages. However, the natural experiment alongside a longitudinal study available to researchers in this case provided useful information about the effectiveness of different types of cigarette package warnings.

Helping to establish causation

Additionally, longitudinal data can help us to establish **causation** in a more robust way than cross-sectional data. A cross-sectional study can show that two variables are related, or correlated, but it cannot tell us whether there is a causal relationship between the two – in other words, whether one of the variables causes changes in the other. It can simply tell us that the variables are correlated. A longitudinal study, on the other hand, can be used to help establish a causal relationship. However, it should be borne in mind that longitudinal studies cannot concretely establish causality, as it may be that a third variable that the researcher has not considered actually caused an outcome. An example of how a longitudinal study has helped us to understand causal relationships between different variables can be seen in the relationship between anxiety, depression and insomnia. Previous research has shown that anxiety and depression are often comorbid (they occur together), and that anxiety may lead to depression, but no study had looked at whether insomnia may be a mediating factor in that relationship. Using data from the National Longitudinal St... to Adult Health in the US (see the study profile in this chapter), da... adolescents across a 14-year period established that anxiety general... leading to depression, but insomnia can be a mediating factor (Li et ...

Research spotlight

Li, Y.I., Starr, L.R. and Wray-Lake, L. (2018) 'I... mediates the longitudinal relationship betwee... depressive symptoms in a nationally represer... of adolescents'

Li and colleagues set out to explore the role that insomnia ... between anxiety and depression in adolescents. They knew th... shown that anxiety and depression were often comorbid co... and that it was likely that anxiety caused depression in a certain... but they wanted to understand whether insomnia could be a fact... mediates, this relationship. To investigate this question, they turne... data in the form of the National Longitudinal Study of Adolescent to A... the US.

What they found was that insomnia does indeed mediate the relationship ... anxiety and depression. Young people with anxiety were more likely to suffe... sleep-related issues, and as sleep problems persist, anxiety over lack of sleep ... emerge. Consequently, individuals with sleep problems are more likely to develo... depression.

This study was only possible through the use of longitudinal data, tracking a large number of adolescents over time, collecting information about their experiences of anxiety, depression and insomnia. It provided important evidence around effective ways of targeting treatment of anxiety in order to prevent future depression.

STUDY PROFILE

The National Longitudinal Study of Adolescent to Adult Health

Established: 1994.

Country: United States.

Sampling unit: individuals.

Sample size at base: 12,105 (core in-home sample at wave 1).

Frequency of interviews: irregular: 1994-5, 1996, 2001-2, 2008, 2016-18.

Participants: adolescents in school grades 7-12 in the 1994-5 school year.

(Continued)

Topics covered: ec... onomic, health, well-being, family, education, relationships, neighbourhood.

Methods of data ... collection: self-completion questionnaires and face-to-face interviews.

...tures: bio-measure collection, data linkage.

...ity: data are available to the research community via the Carolina Population ... Portal.

...rmation: www.cpc.unc.edu/projects/addhealth

...s: what are the drawbacks of longitudinal ...earch?

...pite the large number of advantages of the collection and use of longitudinal data, ...ere are also some drawbacks. While the advantages relate often to the uniqueness ...f the data and its ability to tell us things that cross-sectional data cannot, the disadvantages are often stuck at the data collection stage. However, these disadvantages can also have an impact on the subsequent use of longitudinal data, as we will explore in this section.

Costs associated with tracing

Carrying out a longitudinal study is expensive. As well as the costs associated with carrying out interviews or conducting questionnaires with a group of people every few years, there are additional costs in **tracing**, or tracking, these people over time. The crux of longitudinal research is that the same sample points, usually people or households, continue to take part often over long periods of time, and as such it is crucial to be able to interview them regularly. People often move house, so the study must trace where those people have moved to in an attempt to persuade them to participate again. There are multiple ways of tracking people, as well as methods of reducing the likelihood of failing to locate them.

Prospective methods of participant tracking are those that invite the participant to proactively provide the study with updated contact details – for example, through the use of a telephone line that respondents can call, a study website or change of details cards which respondents can post to the study when they have new contact details – for example, address, telephone number, etc. Studies may also send participants regular requests to update or confirm their contact details, which may be incentivised using cash or vouchers. During an interview, studies may collect the intention of participants to move house and the new address if known.

Once studies have lost contact with a participant, retrospective methods can be used to track them to a new address. There are many options for retrospective tracking:

1. Using directories, such as a telephone book.
2. Using an electoral register or population register if one exists.
3. Using administrative datasets, such as data collected by health services, education providers, or the local or national government.
4. Using social media or other forms of online presence.
5. Contacting relatives of the participant.
6. Contacting the current residents of the last known address of the participant.
7. Contacting people who the study member has given the study details for in the event that they move and cannot be located, often called a 'stable contact'.

Each of these methods requires time, and therefore resources, in order to find participants. Additionally, there may be fees associated with using administrative datasets or other databases. As such, these costs may become very large, particularly for a large study.

Attrition

Attrition – in other words, participants dropping out – can be a drawback of conducting a longitudinal study. It is normal for longitudinal research to experience 'loss' of participants, either because they can no longer be traced by the study, as described above, or because they have refused to participate, or because they have died, or because they are no longer eligible to participate (because they have moved out of the country, for example).

However, once large numbers of people who originally took part no longer participate, a bias may be introduced – that is to say, the sample of people who participate may no longer be **representative** of the population under study, and so research carried out using the data may not come to conclusions that are generalisable to the population. The longer a study continues, the more likely it is that attrition may have introduced bias into the data. More about attrition can be found in Chapter 4.

Participant burden

Participant burden can be an issue with longitudinal studies. Burden can be defined as the degree to which a respondent feels that participating in a survey has been time-consuming, difficult or emotionally challenging. Things that can contribute to a participant feeling burdened are difficult or complex questions, questions about sensitive topics and long interviews (Lavrakas, 2008).

In a longitudinal study, participants are required to take part in the study at multiple points in time, and may be subject to long interviews or other burdensome tasks, like cognitive assessments or bio-measure collection. This may result in the participant feeling burdened, which could lead to a couple of different things. First, they may provide data of lower quality to end an interview or questionnaire quicker. This might be because they don't think about their answers fully, or because they don't give full information because they know it takes time and extends the interview. For example, participants might know from previous experience that if they say they have gained a new qualification since the last interview, they will be asked a number of follow-up questions to capture details about that qualification. As such, rather than say they have gained a new qualification when asked, they might not mention it to avoid the additional questions they know will follow. Alternatively, burden may cause the participant to drop out of the study altogether. With either possibility, bias may be introduced into the data.

However, there are methods for reducing respondent burden, which may encourage longitudinal participants to continue taking part in the study. The majority of these methods focus on reducing the complexity of questions, shortening questionnaires where possible, and breaking up questionnaires into more manageable, enjoyable chunks. However, in cases where burden cannot be reduced, financial incentives are often offered to participants to compensate for the burden they experience as part of a study.

Analytic complexity

The complexity of longitudinal data may pose problems for researchers. Specific analytic techniques must be used in order to account for the fact that data has been collected from the same individuals at more than one point in time. More about analytical techniques appropriate for longitudinal data can be found in Chapter 11.

THEORY OF CHANGE

As well as the practical issues that need to be taken care of when designing a longitudinal study and using longitudinal data, there are also theoretical questions to be considered.

A crucial part of using longitudinal data to study change is developing a theory of change – understanding which variables are of interest to the research and theoretically how they relate, and how change may occur over time. This can be particularly complex when change is dynamic – that is to say, where changes in predictor variables create changes in outcomes, rather than one static level of a predictor equating to a static level of the outcome (Ployhart and Vandenberg, 2010). Put more simply, instead of a simple relationship between variables, where over time variable A (the predictor variable) causes changes to variable B (the outcome variable), in the same way, dynamic change means that as variable A changes in different ways over time, the impact that has on variable B also differs.

In order to understand change, we must take a step back and understand what we mean by the ideas of 'change' and 'time' and how they relate. Time does not generally cause change. Time does not cause us to grow from babies, through childhood and adulthood and into old age. Time is the scale by which we measure this process, or change, but it is not the cause (Wang et al., 2017). Understanding change in this way can then lead us to conduct longitudinal research with one of two aims: either we want to describe changes that occur over time (descriptive research) or we want to explain why change over time has occurred (exploratory research). In each case, we need to begin by developing a theory or hypothesis about what change will look like in the variables of interest.

Forms of change

Change can occur in many different forms, or patterns, generally typified into three categories: linear, non-linear and discontinuous. Each of these forms are described below.

Linear change

Linear change is the most basic, and probably the simplest form of change to understand. This is where, as the independent variable changes by a certain amount, the dependent variable changes by a certain amount. This can be a positive relationship, as seen in Figure 1.1.

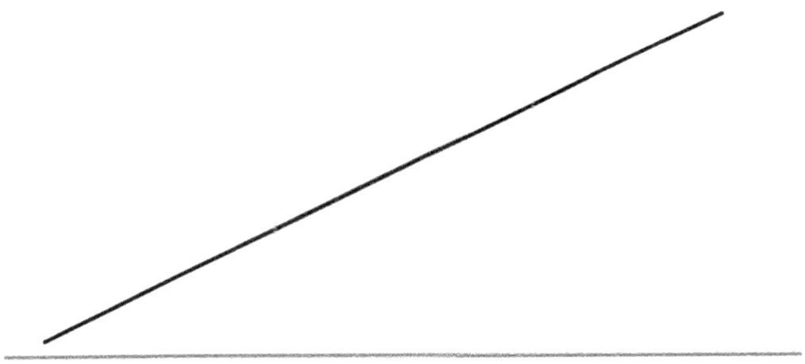

Figure 1.1 An example of a positive linear relationship

It can also be a negative relationship, as shown in Figure 1.2.

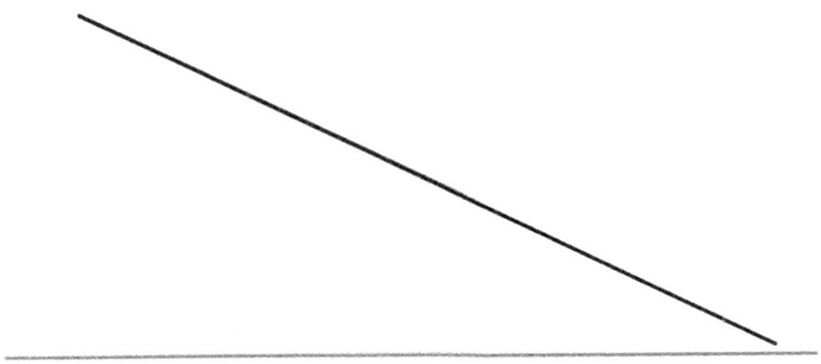

Figure 1.2 An example of a negative linear relationship

An example of a positive linear relationship is between house size and house value. On a particular street, as the size of the house increases, the value of the house also increases in a linear fashion.

Non-linear change

Non-linear change is where changes in the independent variable lead to different amounts of change in the dependent variable, depending on the level of the independent variable – that is to say, change doesn't follow a simple proportional relationship.

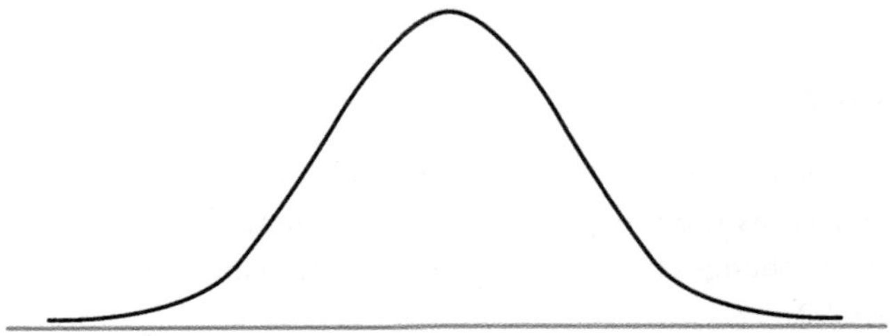

Figure 1.3 An example of a non-linear relationship

The curve in Figure 1.3 could represent the relationship between a particular drug and its ability to help the patient. As the dose of the drug increases, so does its effectiveness. However, at a certain point, as too much of the drug is given, its helpfulness decreases as it begins to harm the patient.

Another example would be a curve with decreasing returns, as shown in Figure 1.4.

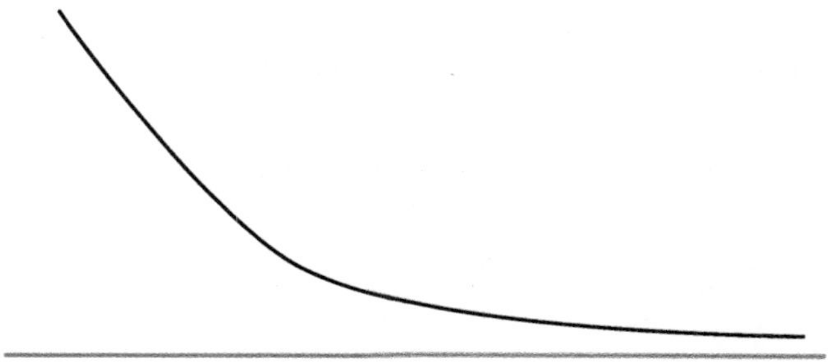

Figure 1.4 An example of a non-linear relationship, in the form of a curve with decreasing returns

If we think about a curve of this shape, we could look at car values. As the age of the car increases, the value of the car (generally) decreases, but a lot of this devaluation occurs in the first few years, with the rate of devaluation tailing off as time goes on.

Discontinuous change

Sometimes the relationship between two variables is not smooth, and there may be a sudden change in the direction of the relationship or a sharp change in trajectory. The change of trajectory is often caused by an external event, such as an intervention programme or an economic crisis.

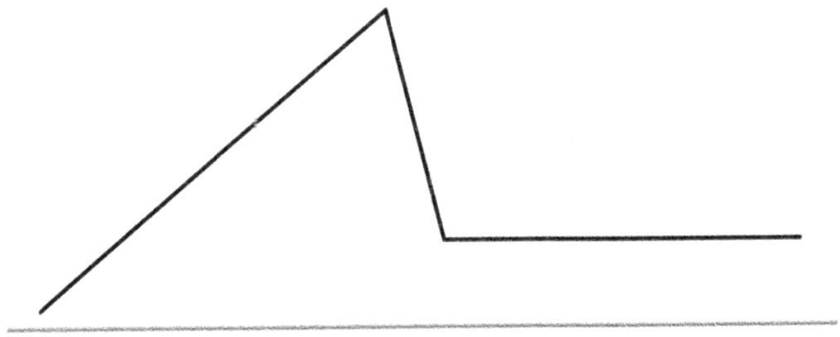

Figure 1.5 An example of a discontinuous change

For example, a relationship with the pattern seen in Figure 1.5 could be between rainfall and water levels in a lake controlled by a dam. As the rainfall increases, so does the level of the lake. However, at some point, it is decided that the dam gates will be opened. As a result, a lot of water is released and the lake level falls, even though it is still raining.

Developing a theory of change - and beyond

Theorising about the relationship between the independent and dependent variables, including the type of change expected, is important when designing research that utilises longitudinal data. This also extends into the consideration of causality.

Taking the idea of developing a theory of change one stage further, it is also important to look beyond the theoretical and towards the practical. This involves choosing longitudinal data pertinent to your theory of change, ensuring that the methodological choices, such as frequency of data collection and number of observations, are appropriate, through to awareness of analytical issues and appropriateness. Ployhart and Vandenberg (2010) offer a helpful checklist of issues to consider when designing longitudinal research or using longitudinal data, framed around the theory of change. This work is helpful not just in terms of study design, but also for researchers wishing to use longitudinal data. Working through the checklist will ensure that researchers think about key issues related to the theory of change. Figure 1.6 takes the key themes of Ployhart and Vandenberg's checklist, framing them as questions for a study designer or researcher to think about. This chapter has already covered many of the theoretical issues, while the following chapters pick up on the methodological and analytical issues in more depth.

Longitudinal study design: issues to consider

Theoretical

- What's your theory of change? Does cross-sectional theory and research give you enough for developing a theory around longitudinal change?
- What do you think the change should look like? Do you have other data sources that show what it looks like?
- What level of change are you interested in? Group average change, individual-level change, or something else?

Methodological

- What is the ideal number of measurements and at what time intervals for you to investigate your theory of change?
- What sample do you need to understand change?
- How many measurement points do you need to collect from each sampling unit? How might attrition affect data collection?
- How are you going to actually measure change over time? What questions or other measures are appropriate?

Analytical

- Is your analytical method appropriate for longitudinal data, and for assessing change?
- What are the strengths/weaknesses of your method for understanding change?
- Have you reported sufficient information to allow readers to understand and evaluate the findings themselves?

Figure 1.6 Issues for consideration when designing or using longitudinal data

Key learning points

- A longitudinal study follows the same sampling units, usually people or households, over time, taking repeated measures.
- Sampling units are chosen to represent a population of interest.
- Longitudinal studies allow us to see how people's situations, behaviours, attitudes and lives change over time, on an individual level.

- Longitudinal research has a number of advantages:
  - understanding how the past shapes the future;
  - getting around the problems of human memory;
  - allowing us to disentangle age, period and cohort effects;
  - taking advantage of natural experiments to assess effectiveness of policy, impact of unexpected events, and so on.
  - Helping to establish causation.
- There are disadvantages to conducting longitudinal studies:
  - they are expensive - there are particularly large costs associated with tracing;
  - attrition (participants dropping out of the study) can cause problems with bias;
  - participants can feel burdened;
  - data analysis is complex.
- It is important to develop a theory of change when using longitudinal data - understanding which variables are of interest to the research, theoretically how they relate and how change may occur over time.
- There are three main forms of change that can occur between variables: linear, non-linear and discontinuous.

Check your understanding

1. Define a sampling unit.
2. Why should a longitudinal study ideally have three or more time points?
3. What does longitudinal data offer over cross-sectional data?
4. Briefly describe three disadvantages of longitudinal studies.
5. List the three forms of change and describe each of them.

WANT TO FIND OUT MORE?

The resources below are great sources of additional information on the content covered in this section.

An introductory learning module about the basics of longitudinal studies by CLOSER in the UK: https://learning.closer.ac.uk/learning-modules/introduction/

An exploration of age, period and cohort effects:

Bell, A. (2020) 'Age period cohort analysis: A review of what we should and shouldn't do', *Annals of Human Biology*, 47 (2): 208–17.

A summary of approaches taken by various longitudinal studies with respect to participant tracing:

Calderwood, L. (2012) 'Tracking sample members in longitudinal studies', *Survey Practice*, 5 (4).

NOTES

1. See Chapter 3 for more information on boost samples.
2. Collection of biological markers, such as blood samples to conduct health assessments.
3. Linking survey data to external data sources, such as health records or tax records, for example.

2

TYPES OF LONGITUDINAL STUDY DESIGNS

OVERVIEW OF CONTENT

This chapter will provide you with information about the main types of longitudinal design. We will look at repeated cross-section designs, retrospective longitudinal studies, prospective longitudinal studies and cohort studies. The benefits and drawbacks of each design will be explored.

As well as overarching study design choices, we will also examine some of the decisions taken by designers which users of longitudinal data need to be aware of and understand. These issues include the **target population** of the study, the study following rules, frequency and method of data collection, and any changes to the sample during the lifetime of the study.

Learning outcomes

After you have read this chapter, you will be able to:

- describe different longitudinal study designs (repeated cross-sections, retrospective longitudinal, prospective longitudinal, and cohort studies);
- understand the benefits and drawbacks of each design;
- understand other important design decisions.

STUDY DESIGNS

There are many different ways that longitudinal studies can be designed. Each bring their own specific benefits, as well as different drawbacks. One of the common benefits between all the different types of longitudinal study is the ability to look at how different things change or stay the same over time at a population level. For example, researchers could look at life satisfaction – how happy or unhappy people report being with their lives. We can see how individual circumstances, life events or experiences impact happiness on an individual level. We can also see whether this changes for a population over a number of years, and even look at whether particular national or global events, such as an economic recession or a global pandemic, affect the happiness of a nation, or whether different cohorts of people are affected in different ways. Chapter 1 provides a fuller discussion of the overarching benefits and drawbacks of longitudinal studies.

Moving beyond the general, understanding the specific design features of a study is crucial to understanding what questions you can ask of the data. The main types of longitudinal study design are described in this chapter, along with their advantages and disadvantages. In addition, the chapter covers additional design issues that need to be considered, beyond simply the type of study.

Repeated cross-sections

Repeated cross-sectional studies ask the same questions to different groups of people at different time points. By design, this type of study may not be considered a 'true' longitudinal study, as it does not follow the same sampling units – for example, people, household, businesses – over time. However, the design still allows us to look at population-level changes over time, making it longitudinal in nature. Figure 2.1 provides a graphical illustration of a repeated cross-sectional study.

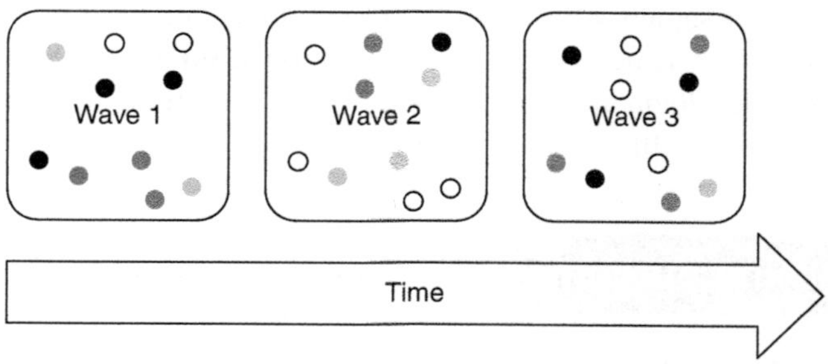

Figure 2.1 A visual representation of a repeated cross-sectional study

Benefits

The major benefit of carrying out a repeated cross-sectional study is that different respondents are interviewed at each time point, meaning that the time, effort and cost required to trace the same individuals over time is removed. This makes this type of study generally much easier and cheaper to run than other types of longitudinal study.

Conducting a survey in this way still allows us to see population-level changes over time, which is a benefit over a survey conducted at a single point in time (a cross-sectional study), which only provides a snapshot of what's happening at a single timepoint.

Drawbacks

While a benefit of a repeated cross-sectional study is that different respondents are interviewed at the different time points, this is also its drawback. As individuals are not followed over time, we are unable to infer anything about change at the individual level. Instead, all that can be assessed is change at the population level. It is possible that while something stays stable in the population, there is a lot of change happening at the individual level. See Chapter 1 for an example of this, looking at poverty.

Examples

There are many examples of repeated cross-sectional studies, from many different fields.

The Public Attitude Survey, a repeated cross-sectional survey carried out by the Mayor's Office for Policing And Crime (MOPAC) in London is one such example. The survey aims to understand people's experiences of, and attitudes towards, policing and crime in London. Instead of following the same participants over time, it interviews a new sample each time. Interviews are constantly ongoing, which means that trends over time can be tracked on a monthly, quarterly or yearly basis. Surveys such as this can be used to understand how perceptions change among a population over time. One such research example was conducted by Hohl and colleagues (2012), which used the Public Attitude Survey data to understand the impact of the 2011 London riots on people's perceptions towards the police.

Research spotlight

Hohl, K., Stanko, B. and Newburn, T. (2012) 'The effect of the 2011 London disorder on public opinion of police and attitudes towards crime, disorder, and sentencing'

Hohl and colleagues used the Public Attitude Survey, a repeated cross-sectional study of Londoners' attitudes towards policing and crime, to look at the effect that the policing of the 2011 riots in London had on perceptions of the police. By comparing data collected before the riots with data collected afterwards, they were able to document the impact on public perceptions and attitudes.

(Continued)

The researchers found that the perceptions of around 25 per cent of Londoners were affected by the riots, with around half of those saying the policing of the riots had improved their opinion of the police and the other half saying that it had got worse. However, when the researchers looked at a measure of confidence in the police, the measure remained stable across the period from before the riots and afterwards. When they looked at geographic areas, they found that when looking at a measure of perception of police effectiveness, this was most likely to have dropped in areas that were worst hit by the riots. The researchers also looked at whether people believe that criminals should receive harsher sentences than they do currently. This measure increased after the riots took place.

This research demonstrates that despite not following the same respondents over time, repeated cross-sectional studies can offer insights into the changing attitudes of a population. While the example looked at the impact of a specific event, it could also be applied more generally to look at changing attitudes and behaviours.

Repeated cross-sectional studies are also the method of choice for a number of studies that aim to collect data on economic and labour-force indicators in particular. The Current Population Survey (CPS) is a monthly survey conducted by the U.S. Census Bureau for the Bureau of Labor Statistics. The CPS interviews around 60,000 households every month, capturing information about employment and unemployment, income and working hours, among other things. Each household is only interviewed once, but by looking at changes in the measures over time, researchers can see how the employment situation in the US is changing at the population level.

STUDY PROFILE

Mayor's Office for Policing And Crime Public Attitude Survey (PAS)

Established: 1983.

Country: England.

Sampling unit: individuals.

Sample size at base: varied.

Frequency of interviews: continuous rolling interviews.

Participants: a random sample of people aged 16+ living in London.

Topics covered: perceptions of the police, trust in the police, perceptions of local neighbourhood, experiences of crime.

Methods of data collection: face-to-face (telephone during the COVID-19 pandemic).

Data availability: data are available via MOPAC.

More information: www.london.gov.uk/what-we-do/mayors-office-policing-and-crime-mopac/data-and-statistics

Retrospective longitudinal studies

Retrospective longitudinal studies follow the same people across a period of time in the way that we usually think of a longitudinal study. In order to be a part of the study, a participant usually must have already experienced a particular life event or belong to a particular category of people – for example, have a particular illness. Figure 2.2 shows a graphical illustration of a repeated cross-sectional study.

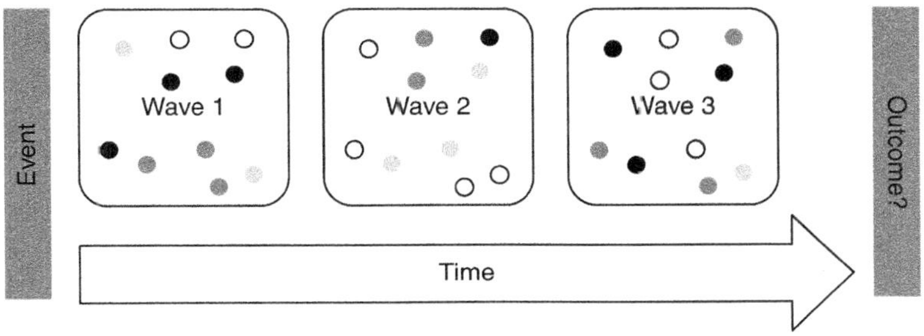

Figure 2.2 A visual representation of a retrospective longitudinal study

Retrospective longitudinal studies tend to be most often used in epidemiology, medical and other health-related fields. Often the event is a medical event or an illness, and the purpose of the study is to assess the factors from an individual's background which may have contributed to the event or illness, and then monitor progress going forward. The study can also see how any interventions given during the course of the study affect the person's outcomes.

There are two main ways in which retrospective longitudinal studies are designed. First, the participants in the study may be asked to provide information (through interviews, questionnaires, etc.) on a regular basis, in the way that we perhaps think of a traditional social sciences study. The second doesn't involve the study member directly providing any information at all. Rather, administrative records are used to follow the progression of the individual without ever having to talk to them. This type of retrospective longitudinal study is more commonly used in epidemiology and other medical studies. Medical records of study members can be obtained on a regular basis, so researchers can follow their diagnosis, treatment and outcomes in a remote way.

Benefits

The first benefit of a retrospective longitudinal study is that individual change can be assessed. By following the same individuals, we can look at how things change not just at a group level, but also for each individual. This allows us deeper insight into how different groups of people may be affected by events and experiences differently.

If the study is set up in a way where records are used, rather than primary data collection with study members, a cost saving can be found – generally interviewing multiple people is far more costly than accessing existing records about them.

Drawbacks

The first drawback, as is seen with so many longitudinal study designs, is that individuals must be followed over time. This takes time and money to do, increasing study costs overall – more so if the individuals are providing primary data. In addition, it is likely that some participants either do not want to take part in the study more than once or over an ongoing period, and some become 'lost' to the study when they can't be traced. The loss of participants in this way can affect the data collected, particularly if certain types of people are more likely to drop out compared with others. An example would be those who are highly mobile. People who move house often are probably different in some ways from those who spend decades living at the same address, and they are also much more likely to become lost to the study. The loss of this particular group of people may affect the results of the study overall.

However, it is possible to **refresh the sample** in this type of study – that is, as people drop out, introduce new participants into the study who fit the same criteria as the original sample. This boosting of numbers helps keep the sample size large enough and potentially representative enough of the population as a whole for meaningful analysis.

The second major area where retrospective longitudinal studies create challenges is due to their retrospective nature. Historical information about the participant is collected often long after the event, with the respondent recalling previous events in their life (unless, of course, the individual is followed via official administrative methods). The human memory is usually imperfect, meaning that when asking respondents to recall things that happened to them many months, years or even decades before, the responses they provide may not always be accurate. Inaccuracy in recall can lead to **bias** in subsequent data. The issues associated with respondent recall are discussed further in Chapter 6.

In addition, attrition can be a problem. At its most simple, attrition is where participants of a study 'drop out' – in other words, they no longer take part in the study. Given that the aim of a study is to follow people over time, this causes a problem because attrition is often not random. Those who no longer take part in a study are usually different from those who remain in the study in some way, and so the sample may no longer be representative of the population of interest. This can be a big problem when using the study data to draw conclusions about the population. Retrospective longitudinal studies that use information from administrative records, rather than directly collection information through surveys, may suffer from attrition to a lesser extent, but it can still be an issue. See Chapter 4 for more information about attrition.

Examples

The Hertfordshire Cohort Study provides a good example of a retrospective longitudinal study. In the 1980s, researchers realised that there was a **correlation** between the rates of death from heart disease in local authority areas and the rates of infant mortality in those areas decades before. This led to the question of whether early life circumstances, including environmental factors, contributed to the development of heart disease years later. As a result, the Hertfordshire Cohort Study was founded. The study found birth records of people born in Hertfordshire in the first part of the twentieth century, then linked those with current records to try to establish the outcomes of those individuals – had they died and, if so, what of, or were they still living? For those who were still living in Hertfordshire, the study sent them letters, asking if they would like to be part of the cohort study. Thus, the study has information from birth on a cohort of individuals, knows the outcomes for those people, and is able to conduct new research with cohort members who are still alive and living in the local area. With regard to the original research question of heart disease, in the early 1990s, a research team published their findings, showing clear links between early life circumstances and outcomes later in life (Osmond et al., 1993), highlighting just how important longitudinal studies are for understanding the influences of early life on later-life outcomes.

Research spotlight

Osmond, C., Barker, D.J.P., Winter, P.D., Fall, C.H.D. and Simmonds, S.J. (1993) 'Early growth and death from cardiovascular disease in women'

Osmond and colleagues used the Hertfordshire Cohort Study to investigate whether they could predict death from cardiovascular disease based on information about pregnancy and early life circumstances. There had already been studies that linked in-utero growth, circumstances of childhood and later development of cardiovascular problems in men, so the authors wanted to find out whether the same links were present for women.

They utilised information available from the Hertfordshire Cohort Study, particularly looking at weight at birth, weight at one year of age and subsequent death from cardiovascular disease. They found that for women, cardiovascular death was predicted more strongly by a below-average weight at birth, but an above-average weight at age one. For men, this was slightly different, with a below-average weight at both birth and age one, predicting subsequent cardiovascular-related death. This showed that while early life circumstances were clearly related to the risk of cardiovascular-related death in later life, men and women were affected by different risk factors in different ways.

This study shows how a retrospective longitudinal study can shed light on how early life circumstances can impact outcomes much later in life. Without this retrospective data, it would have been very difficult to conduct a study into this specific issue.

Numerous other retrospective longitudinal studies exist in the health field, interested in a variety of different outcomes. Bruin-Huisman et al. (2017) have looked at potentially inappropriate prescribing of medication to older patients in the Netherlands to assess the effects on health. They used information routinely collected by GPs in the Netherlands related to 182,000 patients, concluding that potentially inappropriate prescribing was substantial and warranted further investigation.

Lee et al. (2016) used a retrospective longitudinal study to investigate the links between abdominal obesity and shift work in a cohort of 20–39-year-old nurses in Korea. The researchers knew that abdominal obesity was linked to numerous health problems, including diabetes and cardiovascular disease, and that shift work was linked to increased likelihood of suffering from abdominal obesity. Health-screening results that were obtained from nurses on an annual basis were retrospectively analysed to assess the effect of shift working on abdominal obesity. The authors found that nurses who worked shifts were more likely to suffer abdominal obesity, concluding that it would be useful for strategies to be put into place to try to reduce abdominal obesity amongst shift workers in particular.

These examples show that retrospective longitudinal studies can be used to show links between circumstances, actions and outcomes, as well as highlighting social, environmental and medical problems, and exposing gaps in both research and policy that need to be filled.

STUDY PROFILE

Hertfordshire Cohort Study

Established: 1998.

Country: England.

Sampling unit: individuals.

Sample size at base: 2,997.

Frequency of interviews: irregular.

Participants: people born in Hertfordshire in the UK between 1931 and 1939 who were recruited between 1998 and 2004.

Topics covered: birth circumstances, health information, diet, social support and networks.

Methods of data collection: record linkage.

Data availability: via the principal investigator.

More information: www.mrc.soton.ac.uk/herts/

Prospective longitudinal studies

Like retrospective longitudinal studies, **prospective longitudinal studies** follow the same people over time in order to observe behaviours, experiences and attitudes across time. However, unlike retrospective studies, participants have generally not experienced the outcome of interest; they are a (usually random) group of people representing the population who are followed to see what their outcomes are. Figure 2.3 illustrates this approach visually.

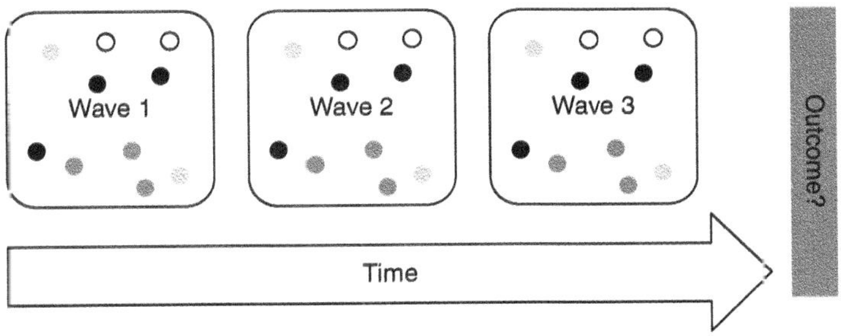

Figure 2.3 A visual representation of a prospective longitudinal study

Benefits

Like retrospective longitudinal studies, prospective longitudinal studies allow researchers to look into individual change, outcomes and causality due to the fact that the same people are followed over time. This allows us deeper insight into how different groups of people may be affected by events and experiences differently, rather than just being able to look at population-level change over time.

In addition, because respondents are often followed from the beginning of the study, and not only after a certain event, they are often not required to provide large amounts of retrospective data. Instead, information is collected on an ongoing basis. This lessens the impact of respondent recall issues.

Drawbacks

However, as with retrospective longitudinal studies, prospective longitudinal studies are often expensive to run as the same group of people have to be tracked and contacted across often long periods of time.

Attrition can also be a problem, whereby respondents stop taking part in the study. When those who drop out are different from those who remain in the study, the sample representativeness drops, meaning that the data produced by the study may no longer be effective or accurate in drawing conclusions about the population of interest.

As well as this, it can take a long time to collect the volume of data that allows certain research questions to be answered. If researchers are interested in how early life experiences affect outcomes later in life, there may need to be data available that spans many years or even decades. As such, these studies are a huge investment and only reach their full potential many years after inception.

Examples

There are a large number of prospective longitudinal studies worldwide. In the UK, the UK Household Longitudinal Study (Understanding Society) is the biggest, following around 40,000 households across time (see Chapter 1 for a summary of Understanding Society). In the US, the Panel Study of Income Dynamics (PSID) is the longest running longitudinal household survey in the world, having been set up in the 1960s. Such a wealth of data has led to large amounts of research using the study's data. Due to the fact the PSID contains multiple generations of the same family, work around intergenerational transmission has been possible. One such example is a study by Davis and colleagues (2015), looking at obesity across multiple generations.

Research spotlight

Davis, M.M., McGonagle, K., Schoeni, R.F. and Stafford, F. (2015) 'Grandparental and parental obesity influences on childhood overweight: Implications for primary care practice'

Davis et al. set out to look at some of the factors that influence whether a child is overweight - specifically, whether a parent or grandparent is also overweight. There had been some work previously that looked at whether the weight status of a parent influenced the likelihood of their child being overweight, but data from the Panel Study of Income Dynamics (PSID) in the United States allowed them to extend this analysis to include grandparents.

They found, in agreement with previous work, that the weight status of a parent is linked to their child's weight. However, the rich data from PSID also allowed them to see that whether or not a grandparent is obese can also have an influence on the child's weight, independent of what the child's parents weigh. This was the first national study to be able to examine this issue.

The research highlighted the need for primary care physicians in particular to take into account grandparents' weight status when looking at whether a child is at risk of becoming overweight. The study demonstrates the importance of rich longitudinal data for being able to conduct relevant, robust research which can feed into policy.

STUDY PROFILE

Panel Study of Income Dynamics (PSID)

Established: 1968.

Country: United States.

Sampling unit: households.

Sample size at base: c. 5,000 households, c. 18,000 individuals.

Frequency of interviews: annually until 1997, then biannually since.

Participants: families living in the United States.

Topics covered: dynamics of income and poverty, health, wealth, expenditure, philanthropy, child development, transition to adulthood.

Methods of data collection: face-to-face.

Innovative features: numerous supplemental studies.

Data availability: data are available to the research community via the University of Michigan Institute for Social Research Survey Research Center's Data Center.

More information: https://psidonline.isr.umich.edu/

Cohort studies

Cohort studies are a special type of prospective longitudinal study. These studies follow a group of people over time who all share a particular characteristic. Most commonly these are birth cohorts, where individuals were all born in the same year, but they could also be a group of people who graduated from high school or university in the same year or worked for a particular company at a certain time, for example. Figure 2.4 provides a visual illustration of a cohort study.

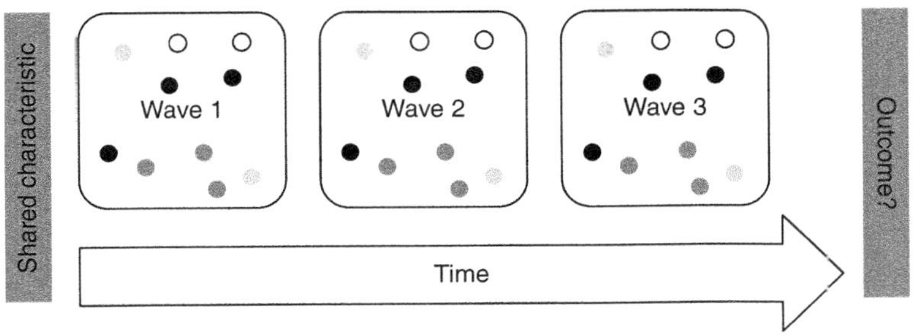

Figure 2.4 A visual representation of a cohort study

Benefits

As with most other longitudinal study designs, cohort studies benefit from being able to look at individual change, rather than just trends over time at a population level. A benefit over other types of longitudinal study is that cohort comparisons can be conducted. Comparing different cohorts can allow researchers to see how things change over time or stay the same, for different groups of people. For example, in the UK, there are four birth cohort studies that track four groups of people who were all born in different years: the National Survey of Health and Development (tracking people born in 1946), the National Child Development Study (following a group of people born in 1958), the 1970 British Cohort Study and the Millennium Cohort Study (following a group of people born at the beginning of the twenty-first century). By comparing the experiences and outcomes of these different cohorts of individuals, we can start to disentangle age, period and cohort effects (see Chapter 1), looking at how their experiences across the life-course are similar or different from each other at different points in time.

Drawbacks

Cohort studies, like other study designs that follow the same people over a period of time, are often expensive to run due to the costs associated with tracing people over time. Unlike other designs, it may also be more difficult to 'refresh' the sample if lots of study members are lost to follow up. For example, the 1970 British Cohort Study aimed to recruit every single person born in Great Britain in a single week in 1970. As such, the entire population of interest was invited to participate in the study. If too many people drop out, there are no other eligible people who could participate instead.

In addition, it can take a long time to collect data that is widely used by researchers to carry out depth analysis. The more data that are collected, the more useful it can become, but obviously if researchers want to look at whether circumstances in childhood affect later outcomes in life – for example, the study would have to have been running for decades in order to have all the information needed for such analysis.

Examples

As mentioned above, the UK has a rich tradition of cohort studies, with four national birth cohorts tracking different groups of people from birth to death. Cross-cohort comparison has enabled researchers to investigate a multitude of facets of life, to see how they have changed or stayed the same for different generations in the UK. One such example is a study by Collishaw and colleagues (2010), which focuses on mental health among adolescents.

Research spotlight

Collishaw, S., Maughan, B., Natarajan, L. and Pickles, A. (2010) 'Trends in adolescent emotional problems in England: A comparison of two national cohorts twenty years apart'

Using data from the 1970 British Cohort Study and the Health Survey for England (a repeated cross-sectional study), Collishaw and colleagues sought to investigate whether emotional problems in adolescence had stayed the same, improved or become worse over time. The two studies both interviewed participants at age 16 (1986 for the

BCS70 cohort and 2006 for the Health Survey for England participants) and asked comparable questions pertaining to emotional issues. This allowed a direct comparison of the two groups of adolescents 20 years apart.

The research found that over time, the prevalence of emotional issues among adolescents had increased. In 2006, twice as many young people reported symptoms of depression or anxiety as they had done in 1986. The researchers were also able to look at a range of demographic and family variables to see whether changes in these things over time may have led to the increases seen in emotional problems, but concluded that these factors did not account for the increased observation of emotional problems. They concluded that the study provided evidence for a rise in emotional problems in young people between 1986 and 2006, particularly among girls.

Cohort studies and other studies allow us to isolate a particular cohort (as the Health Survey for England does) and allow researchers to analyse trends over time, flagging areas where policy intervention may be needed

Another special group of cohort studies are those that follow people who were born at the turn of the twenty-first century. Across the world there are cohort studies that have been set up to follow people born around the year 2000. These studies exist in the UK, Ireland, France, Australia and New Zealand, to name but a few. As more and more data are collected, the studies will become more and more useful to understand the experiences of a generation across the world. They will be invaluable to compare how experiences of the same generation differ in different situations around the world, as well as being used for within-country comparisons with studies of different generations.

STUDY **PROFILE**

1970 British Cohort Study (BCS70)

Established 1970.

Country: England, Scotland and Wales.

Sampling unit: individuals.

Sample size at base: c. 17,000.

Frequency of interviews: irregular.

Participants: every baby born in Great Britain in a single week in 1970.

Topics covered: health, physical development, education, social development, economic circumstances.

Methods of data collection: face-to-face primarily, but also paper questionnaires, telephone and online interviews.

Innovative features: data linkage, bio-measure collection.

Data availability: data are available to the research community via the UK Data Archive.

More information: https://cls.ucl.ac.uk/cls-studies/1970-british-cohort-study/

STUDY **PROFILE**

The Longitudinal Study of Australian Children (LSAC), also known as Growing Up in Australia

Established: 2004.

Country: Australia.

Sampling unit: individuals.

Sample size at base: c. 10,000 individuals, split across two cohorts.

Frequency of interviews: every two years.

Participants: 5,000 children born in 2000, 5,000 children born in 2003, along with their resident and non-resident parents, carers and teachers.

Topics covered: development, housing, finances, health, education, relationships.

Methods of data collection: face-to-face primarily, but also paper questionnaires, telephone and online interviews.

Innovative features: data linkage, bio-measure collection.

Data availability: data are available to the research community via the National Centre for Longitudinal Data's Dataverse.

More information: https://growingupinaustralia.gov.au/about-study

Design choices

As well as the design of the study in terms of choosing between different types of longitudinal study – for example, retrospective, cohort, etc. – there are a number of other design choices that need to be made. Understanding these design choices helps the researcher to understand exactly how data were collected, which is essential when carrying out analysis of the data. This section explores some of these design choices and highlights why each may be important for a researcher to understand prior to conducting analysis.

Who is the target population?

It is crucial to understand the target population – the group of people that the study aims to represent. Many of the studies mentioned so far in this book are representative of the population of a country – that is to say, results from the study, if analysis is carried out correctly, can be applied to the population level with reasonable confidence. However, some studies only represent people from smaller geographic areas and some only capture people with certain characteristics or experiences. Before using a longitudinal dataset, the researcher must be clear who the target population of the study were and therefore who their results are generalisable to.

Who is followed?

The choice of who a longitudinal study follows can have implications for how the study is carried out, but also what sort of data are available. The two main choices usually preferred in terms of who a study follows are either individuals or households. If a study follows an individual, then it is generally only that person who is interviewed across the life of a study. Other people close to that person, such as partners or children, are not routinely included in data collection. This can have implications for the types of data available and also what can be done with it.

If a study chooses to follow households, things can become more complicated. A household may contain two parents and their children, in which case all members of the household (or perhaps people in the household over a certain age) are interviewed. Once the children grow up and leave the household, they may form a new household, which is also now included in the study. Perhaps the parents separate and form separate households, in which case both households may be followed by the study. Maybe two individuals who are part of the study move into the same house together. Now two households have become one. Keeping track of these households and being clear about who is followed can be quite tricky. This is also true of the data produced – understanding the rules around who forms part of the sample and how households have changed over time is key to understanding the data and subsequent use of it.

How often are data collected?

The frequency of data collection is important for understanding the types of research question that can and cannot be asked of the data. Some studies carry out interviews very regularly – for example, maybe every month in terms of some labour force surveys. Others, like the UK Household Longitudinal Study, collect data annually. The British Birth Cohort Studies, on the other hand, interview cohort members once every few years, often when the cohorts are at an age which is considered to be of scientific importance. This is important in reducing participant burden: participants who feel a study is asking too much of them in terms of time or effort may be more likely to drop out, or attrit, which can lead to the study sample becoming less representative, leading to problems with drawing conclusions about the population from the data. More on attrition can be found in Chapter 4.

Researchers should be mindful that a study that only interviews every few years, for example, may not be the best source of information to answer research questions for which it is crucial to know about change or continuity on a very granular level, or for research questions where the outcome of interest changes very frequently. However, for asking questions related to major life events or life-long outcomes, they may be perfectly suitable.

How are data collected?

There are many different methods, or **modes**, used to collect data, be it face-to-face interviews, telephone interviews, paper questionnaires or online surveys. Each mode has advantages and drawbacks (discussed further in Chapters 8 and 9). Knowing how the data were collected allows the researcher to understand the benefits of using said data, but also where the data may not be quite as good.

In addition, if a researcher is interested in comparing different data sources, it may appear on the surface that two different studies that ask participants the same question would be perfect for comparison. However, if one study used face-to-face interviews and the other used a web survey to collect the data, the researcher should be mindful of **mode effects** – in other words, the effect the type of interviewing might have had on the responses given to different questions. See Chapters 8, 9 and 10 for more information on mode effects.

Are the same data collected each time?

If researchers want to look at how things change or stay the same over time, it is important to look at exactly what was asked by the study at each time point. Some studies only ask about certain topics every so often, rather than at every interview. Additionally, the phrasing of a question can change over time within a study. Sometimes even small changes in wording can cause differences in how respondents answer questions, so where it looks like change has occurred in the outcome of interest, it might not be true change but rather the product of changing the wording of the question. An example of this can be found in an experiment on question wording in the General Social Survey in the US (Smith, 1984).

Research spotlight

Smith, T.W. (1984) 'A preliminary analysis of methodological experiments on the 1984 GSS'

As part of the 1984 General Social Survey (GSS) in the US, a number of methodological experiments were embedded. One of these looked at how apparently subtle changes in question wording impacted on responses.

The question of interest was around welfare spending. The question traditionally carried in the GSS asked about government spending priorities, with one of the target concepts being 'welfare'. The team carrying out the survey were concerned that the word 'welfare' might have negative connotations, so used three different versions of the welfare response option in an experiment. One group received the traditional 'welfare' concept, the second group were asked instead about 'assistance to the poor' and the third group received the option 'caring for the poor'. While it could be assumed these were asking about the same assistance programme, respondents viewed them very differently, impacting on responses. A total of 24 per cent said they supported 'welfare', compared with 62 per cent for 'assistance to the poor' and 68 per cent for 'caring for the poor'.

This study demonstrates that even seemingly small wording changes in a question can impact heavily on responses. When looking at longitudinal data, researchers should carefully examine the questions from one time point to the next to ensure that they are comparable over time.

Has the sample been refreshed or boosted?

If many people drop out of a longitudinal study, eventually the sample may be too small or too unrepresentative to conduct meaningful analysis. A solution to this may be to refresh the sample – in other words, recruit more people to the study who meet the original sample criteria. For some studies this is not possible, perhaps because everyone eligible to be in the study was invited to take part at the outset. Alternatively, it may be decided that it is not worth recruiting new people because it is simply not possible to collect the rich history of data that exists for the rest of the sample.

Another reason a longitudinal study sample might include additional participants is to over-sample particular groups of people – for example, if there is research or policy interest in a particular group. These additional samples, or over-samples, are often referred to as '**boost samples**'. A boost sample might contain people who live in particular geographic areas, such as ethnic minorities or immigrants, for example.

If a sample has been refreshed or boosted, users of the data should be aware of this as they may need to account for this in their analysis. For example, if historical data is being used, some respondents will have gaps for this as they weren't part of the study when the data were originally collected. It may also be the case that if the analysis is interested in a representative sample of the population, weighting may need to be applied to account for boost samples. See Chapter 4 for more information about missing data and weighting.

CONCLUSIONS

In order to analyse longitudinal data, there are a number of things you need to understand about the design of the study. First, you will need to know what the overarching study design is – are the same people followed over time or is the sample newly recruited at each timepoint? In addition to these questions, there are many other design decisions that would have been made when the study was conceived. Understanding who the study represents, who is followed and the intricacies of the study design are crucial to being able to understand what questions you can ask of the data.

Key learning points

- There are four main longitudinal study designs: repeated cross-sections, retrospective longitudinal, prospective longitudinal and cohort studies.
- Repeated cross-sectional studies do not follow the same respondents over time; instead, they repeat the same questionnaire over time, drawing different samples of participants for each timepoint.
    - Benefits: they are cheaper and easier to run as the same participants do not have to be followed over time.
    - Drawbacks: they are unable to look at change at the individual level.
- Retrospective longitudinal studies follow the same people across a period of time. In order to be a part of the study, a participant usually must have already experienced a particular life event or belong to a particular category of people. Data are then usually collected about the participant's history - hence, 'retrospective'.
    - Benefits: they are able to look at change at the individual level.
    - Drawbacks: following the same participants over time is expensive. Asking respondents to recall things that happened to them a long time before may not result in accurate data.
- Prospective longitudinal studies also follow the same people over time in order to observe behaviours, experiences and attitudes across time, ultimately to see what their outcomes are. However, participants have generally not experienced an outcome of interest and instead are followed to see what their outcomes are.
    - Benefits: they are able to look at change at the individual level. Collecting data regularly over time lessens respondent recall problems.
    - Drawbacks: issues with following the same respondents over time. Additionally, attrition can be a problem, reducing the representativeness of the data. It can also take a long time to collect data that is able to be used to answer certain questions.
- Cohort studies are a special type of prospective longitudinal study. These studies follow a group of people over time who all share a particular characteristic.
    - Benefits: they are able to look at change at the individual level. By comparing the experiences and outcomes of different cohorts of individuals, we can start to disentangle age, period and cohort effects, looking at how people's experiences across the life-course are similar or different from each other at different points in time.
    - Drawbacks: following the same respondents over time is expensive. Attrition can be a problem. It can take many years to collect enough data to answer certain research questions.
- As well as deciding the overarching design of a longitudinal study, there are other design decisions that need to be taken and also considered when planning to analyse longitudinal data.
    - Who is followed.
    - How often data are collected.
    - The method used to collect data.
    - What data are collected at each timepoint.
    - How to handle the sample once respondents start to drop out.

Check your understanding

1. Briefly describe a repeated cross-sectional study and describe its benefits.
2. What are the differences between a retrospective and prospective longitudinal study?
3. What are the benefits and drawbacks of a cohort study?
4. Name three other design considerations for a longitudinal study, beyond the overarching design.
5. Why should researchers check the wording of questions between different sweeps of a study if they are planning to use the question in longitudinal analysis?

WANT TO FIND OUT MORE?

The resource below is a great source of additional information on the content covered in this section.

Menard, S. (2007) *Handbook of Longitudinal Research*. New York: Academic Press.

3

UNDERSTANDING THE SAMPLE

OVERVIEW OF CONTENT

This chapter covers sampling in a longitudinal context. Starting with basics, it explores what a sample is and why we use them. It will then discuss a number of specific sampling methods, both probability and non-probability, and the benefits and drawbacks of each.

The chapter will also cover refreshment and boost samples, both of which are unique to longitudinal studies. Finally, we will touch on sampling error and the impact on subsequent data analysis.

Learning outcomes

After you have read this chapter, you will be able to:

- describe different methods of probability sampling, their advantages and their drawbacks;
- describe different methods of non-probability sampling, their advantages and their drawbacks;
- understand what over-sampling, boost samples and refreshment samples are;
- understand what sampling error is and how to reduce the likelihood of it occurring.

WHAT IS A SAMPLE?

When looking to use longitudinal data, it is vital to understand the details of the sample the study is using. Let's go back to basics: what is a **sample**? A sample is a group of people, households or other entities of interest that belong to the population that is under study. The aim of the sample in most cases is that it represents the population of interest accurately – in other words, it's representative. If the sample of a study achieves representativeness, it means that research findings from the study can be applied to the population of interest and we can be confident in doing that.

Why use a sample? Why not just talk to everyone in the population we are interested in? In many cases, studies aim to gather information about populations that are very large, such as all adults resident in a country, or everyone in a country who has experienced a health event such as a heart attack, for example. If we wanted to speak to everyone in the whole population, it would take an extremely long time and be very expensive. Instead, we draw a sample of people who represent that population and use the data they provide to draw conclusions about the whole population.

There are some key questions it is important to answer about the sample of a longitudinal study before the data are used for analysis in order to ensure that any analysis carried out is appropriate. These are:

- Who was the population of interest – or target population – of the study?
- How was the sample drawn?
- Was the sample refreshed?
- Was the sample boosted?
- What can I infer about **sampling error**?

This chapter will explore each of these questions in turn, in the sections below.

WHO WAS THE POPULATION OF INTEREST FOR THE STUDY?

When using **secondary data sources**, you should bear in mind the population from which the sample was drawn and make sure it matches your population of interest. For example, perhaps you're interested in working-age adults in a particular country, but the dataset you're using is all residents aged 15 or over.

If the population of interest of the research doesn't match the target population of the dataset you're using, then it may not be possible to infer results from the research to the population of interest of the research. Alternatively, you may have to focus on certain portions only of the study sample, rather than analysing the whole sample. While this seems very basic, it's important to check what the target population of the study you're using is.

HOW WAS THE SAMPLE DRAWN?

It is important to understand how the sample members of a study were chosen for inclusion. There are a number of different ways a sample might be drawn, and it is important to understand the implications of each method on the data that is collected by the study. It is particularly important to know how the sample was drawn when it comes to analysis. Different analysis methods have different assumptions about how sampling units are structured. If these assumptions are violated, then the method will not be appropriate to use. Researchers should pay close attention to this when choosing which methods to use to analyse secondary data. More about longitudinal analysis methods can be found in Chapter 11. The main types of sampling method are discussed in the subsections below, split into probability (random) and non-probability (non-random) sampling methods.

Probability sampling methods

At its most basic, a **probability sample** is one in which the probability of any individual sampling unit included in the sample is known already. The probability does not have to be equal for all sampling units, but it has to be known. The benefit of probability sampling methods is that the sample ultimately selected is likely to be representative of the population of interest. This creates **external validity**, where inferences can be made from the sample to the population as a whole. However, in order to create a probability sample, a **sampling frame** is necessary – that is to say, at some level information on all potential respondents must be available. The information need not necessarily be detailed – it could simply be an electoral register, or a list of all households, or even all addresses in the population – but it must be known. The majority of longitudinal studies employ random sampling methods to ensure that the study is representative of the population of interest. There are a number of different probability sampling methods, which are described below.

Simple random sample

A **simple random sample** is a sampling method by which each of the sampling units (people or households, for example) have an equal chance of being chosen; all sample members are chosen completely at random. Figure 3.1 depicts this visually.

The major advantage of using a simple random sample is that if it is of large enough size, it should create a sample that is representative of the population from which it was drawn. This means that any findings of a survey should be unbiased (notwithstanding the introduction of other errors) and therefore be generalisable to the population as a whole.

However, if the sample size isn't large enough, an error may be introduced. For example, if you were interested in a country's population where the ratio of people

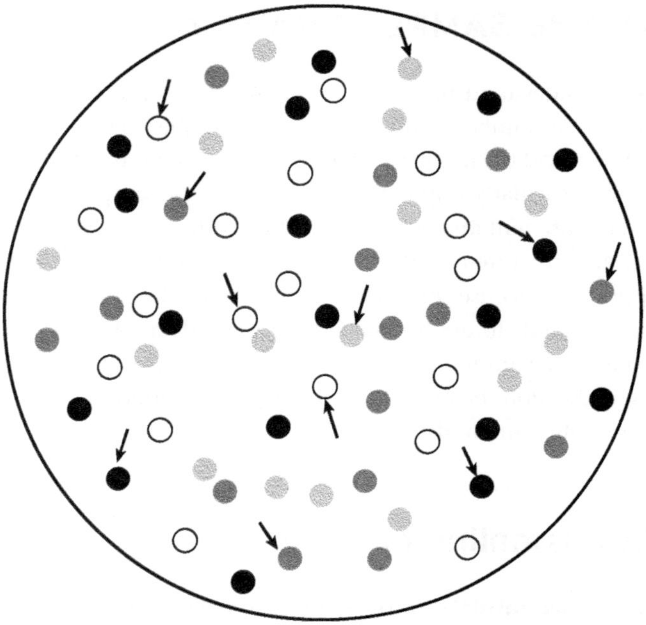

Figure 3.1 A visual representation of a simple random sample

living in a single-person household versus a household with two or more people was 50/50, but you drew a really small sample (say, 100 people), it is possible that you would quite by chance get a split of 70 per cent of people living in single-person households and 30 per cent living in multiple-person households. This is obviously not representative and would be the result of sampling error. We will learn more about sampling error and the consequences later in this chapter.

Additionally, for the data to be representative, there needs to have been a good response rate. So, while the sample itself may be representative, the subsequent data may not be if large numbers of people, or certain groups of people, have not provided data.

There is also the disadvantage of using simple random sampling in terms of practicalities. If a survey is conducted face-to-face, there is likely to be huge geographic spread of participants. This means that interviewers will likely have to travel large distances to reach each participant, driving up the costs of the survey. As a result of this practicality, many face-to-face surveys choose to use slightly different probability sampling methods, as we will see.

Clustered sampling

A **clustered sample** is a sampling method where the population of interest is divided into different groups, called clusters, and then a sample of those groups is drawn. From within these clusters, the researcher usually then selects a final sample of sampling units, perhaps using simple random sampling (as explained above). The clusters could be geographic areas, like towns or cities or groups of schools in a particular area, for example. Generally, the aim of a cluster sample is that each of the clusters are **homogeneous** (i.e., similar to each other), but within each cluster, there is heterogeneity (differences between sampling units). This effectively means that each cluster should on its own roughly represent the population of interest. There are circumstances where clusters are **heterogeneous** – for example, if clusters are geographic across a country and some are in large urban areas, while others are in small rural communities – but the collection of clusters should still be representative as a whole. Figure 3.2 illustrates a clustered sample.

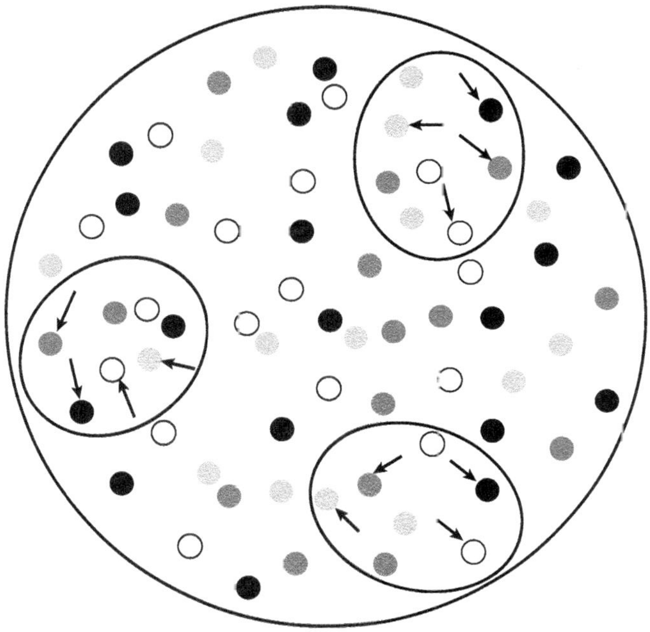

Figure 3.2 A visual representation of a clustered sample

An advantage of using a clustered sample is that data collection may be more productive or efficient. Imagine that you're interested in interviewing a representative sample of a particular country. If a simple random sample was used, interviewees would likely be spread geographically throughout the whole country. Sending interviewers to every sample member would likely be very costly because of the distance between them, and therefore the travel time and cost involved. If instead interviewees were clustered in small geographic areas, each interviewer would be able to effectively and efficiently work in a small area, cutting down on travelling and costs, but retaining a sample that is likely to be representative of the entire population.

However, there is a drawback to using this sampling method. It is likely that sampling error is higher than that seen when a simple random sample is used. Sampling error is described in more detail later in this chapter, but in essence, if the people within a cluster are too similar to one another, error is introduced. One way to reduce this effect is to choose a larger number of clusters, each containing smaller numbers of sampling units.

Additionally, a slight drawback of a clustered sample comes when it is time to analyse data collected from respondents using this method. Unlike a simple random sample, where every member of the population has an equal likelihood of being included in the sample, members of a clustered sample have unequal probabilities of selection. This is because if an individual is not within a cluster that is selected during the first stage of sampling, they have zero probability of being within the second stage, where sampling units are selected. Additionally, there may be another complication if clusters are of different sizes, or if different proportions of sampling units are selected from within each cluster. While this isn't ultimately a problem, it does mean that **weighting** should be applied to ensure that the analysis of data from the sample represents the population of interest. More on weighting can be found in Chapter 4.

An example of a longitudinal study that employed a clustered sampling method is Growing Up in New Zealand, which follows a cohort of children born in New Zealand in 2009–10. In order to select the sample for the study, researchers first selected three geographic areas and then invited all expectant mothers in those areas with an estimated due date between two particular dates in 2009 and 2010 to participate. The rationale for the study using a clustered sampling method was that people within those clusters should be broadly generalisable to the population of New Zealand as a whole (particularly in terms of ethnicity and parental socioeconomic status), but collecting data from within clusters would be more efficient than sending interviewers out across the whole country (Morton et al., 2010).

STUDY PROFILE

Growing Up in New Zealand

Established: 2009.

Country: New Zealand.

Sampling unit: individuals.

Sample size at base: over 6,000.

Frequency of interviews: irregular: multiple data collections spanning from antenatal to latest collection aged 8.

Participants: children born in New Zealand across 2009 and 2010.

Topics covered: early life, education, health and well-being, culture, identity.

Methods of data collection: face-to-face, telephone and web.

Innovative features: anthropometric assessments (measurement/assessment of proportions of the human body such as height or weight).

Data availability: data are available to the research community through a Data Access Application system.

More information: www.growingup.co.nz

Stratified sampling

A **stratified sample** is similar in theory to a clustered sample, where the population of interest is divided into different groups and then individuals within those groups are sampled, but for this method those groups are based on some common characteristics which may be of interest to the research. Each group is referred to as a '**strata**'. This sampling method, in effect, creates subgroups of respondents who are similar to one another on one or more variables. An example of this is research on income. If you are interested in how people with different incomes vary on one or more other measures, you could create strata based on income. People are put into a strata with other people with similar income levels and then a sample is selected from within each strata. This ensures that the resulting sample contains people from different income levels. Figure 3.3 illustrates a stratified sample.

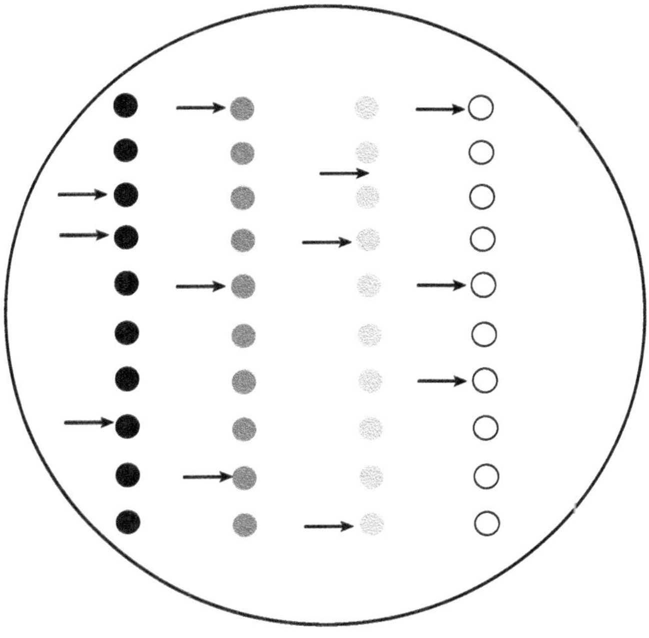

Figure 3.3 A visual representation of a stratified sample

The benefit of using this method is that, as alluded to above, you can ensure that the sample varies on a variable that you are interested in and all levels of that variable are represented in the sample. In addition, you can also ensure that people from small groups in the population are represented. Using other sampling methods, uncommon subgroups may not be adequately represented. An example might be research interested in religion. If you took a simple random sample, you may end up with very few individuals who belong to a particular religion with very few members. If you stratify the sample, you can ensure that each religious group is adequately represented for analysis. This ensures external validity – results can be generalised from the sample taken to the entire population of interest.

However, stratified sampling can be difficult to achieve if the researcher doesn't have access to an adequate sampling frame. In order to be able to create a stratified sample, you need information up front about particular characteristics of the sampling units you want to sample from. Going back to our example of religion, you would need to have details of individuals who are eligible to be included in the sample, which would include their religious affiliation. This may be difficult to achieve.

An example of a longitudinal study that employed stratified sampling to achieve their sample is the Nihon University Longitudinal Study of Aging (NUJLSOA). NUJLSOA is a longitudinal study of adults aged 65 and over in Japan. In order to draw their sample, the study stratified based on geographic region. In Japan, there are 47 prefectures, which were stratified into 11 different regions. The 3,000 municipalities within these regions were then stratified based on population size within each region. From this ordered list, 340 municipalities were then selected by using a systematic sampling method. This means that every 'nth' municipality was selected, ensuring a good spread of municipalities of different sizes. From within each of the 340 municipalities, individuals were then selected to be part of the sample, using different sampling frames. This ensured a good spread of respondents from different types of municipalities – large, small and everything in between.

STUDY PROFILE

Nihon University Longitudinal Study of Aging (NUJLSOA)

Established: 2009.

Country: Japan.

Sampling unit: individuals.

Sample size at base: 4,997.

Frequency of interviews: biannually: 1999, 2001, 2003.

Participants: adults aged 65+ in Japan.

Topics covered: health, mental health, physical functioning, health-related behaviours, family circumstances, socioeconomic variables.

Methods of data collection: face-to-face.

Data availability: data are available to the research community through a Data Access Application system.

More information: https://gero.usc.edu/cbph/nujlsoa/

Non-probability sampling methods

Where probability sampling methods ensure that the probability of selection into the sample for each sampling unit is known, a **non-probability sample** cannot achieve this.

This means that it is difficult to assess how well results from research conducted with a non-probability sample can be inferred from the population of interest as a whole. However, a benefit is that a non-probability sample is often easier, quicker and cheaper to obtain. Additionally, for some research topics, a non-probability sample may be a better way to access a very particular group of people who are of interest. The main non-probability sampling methods are described below.

Quota sampling

To create a **quota sample**, the researcher first thinks about what types of people they want to include in their sample and then they create targets for numbers or proportions of those types of people who should be included in the sample. For example, if you're looking to create a sample that reflects the characteristics of a particular population, you might ensure that your sample contains a reflective range of genders, a range of people in different age groups and people of different ethnicities. If you don't have information about the potential sample beforehand, you can ask questions at the time of recruitment about these characteristics and include individuals in the sample who fit into these certain pre-specified groups.

The benefit of a quota sample is that the sample achieved may reflect the population of interest to some degree, based on the characteristics chosen for the quota. This means that it may be possible to infer the population of interest from the sample (although probably with less confidence than you could for a probability sample). Additionally, it may be much quicker and cheaper to achieve a sample. Probability samples require a sampling frame up front, which may have a cost associated with it. Using a quota sample eliminates the need for a sampling frame.

A drawback is that there might be a key characteristic of interest that isn't included in the original quota. For example, while the sample may represent the population as a whole in terms of gender, ethnicity and age, it might be that income levels of the sample don't match the population. Therefore, results from subsequent research may not be applicable to the population.

Snowball sampling

A **snowball sample**, sometimes called a respondent-driven sample, is a good sampling method to reach minority groups in a population or groups of people who wouldn't usually participate in research studies. To create a snowball sample, the researcher would find a few people they are interested in and include them in the sample. They would then ask them if they knew other people who would also fit the group of interest and would contact them, inviting them to join the sample. Given that people often know other people who are like them in some way, snowball sampling can be an effective recruitment method. An example of a research topic where snowball sampling could work well is research on drug users. A random sample may not include very many people who use drugs, so it would be difficult to draw any conclusions about drug users from a random sample. Instead, a snowball sample could be created. The researcher would find a handful of people who are drug users and ask them if they knew other drug users who might be willing to join the sample. Each of the new recruits to the sample would be asked the same question, creating an ever-larger sample, where each sample member fits the requirement for inclusion in the sample.

The major drawback of this sampling method is the potential lack of representativeness and therefore generalisability. It is not an effective method to create a sample that is representative of a general population. However, for specialised populations, it can work very effectively.

Returning to our example on drug use, this is drawn from a real-life longitudinal study conducted in the United States. Researchers were interested in following a group of Mexican American non-injecting heroin users to understand risk factors for making a transition from non-injecting to injecting (Cepeda and Valdez, 2010). More information on this study can be found in the box below.

Research spotlight

Cepeda, A. and Valdez, A. (2010) 'Ethnographic strategies in the tracking and retention of street-recruited community-based samples of substance using hidden populations in longitudinal studies'

Cepeda and Valdez set out to understand the incidence and risk factors for transitioning from being a non-injecting heroin user to an injecting user, as well as understanding the incidence of blood-borne and sexually transmitted infections among this group. They wanted to recruit a group of non-injecting heroin users and conduct an interview with them, and then conduct follow-up interviews after six and twelve months. They set out some inclusion criteria for sample members (aged 16-40 for females, aged 16-35 for males; evidence of heroin use in the past 30 days; non-injecting drug use or no injected drugs taken in the past 30 days; Mexican American ethnic background; no drug treatment in a formal setting in the past 30 days; and resident of the San Antonio area of Texas), and then went about recruiting participants.

To recruit the sample, the researchers first started looking at areas of San Antonio where people were known to buy or use drugs. On multiple occasions, at different times of the day and on different days of the week they visited those sites, trying to build relationships with people who could potentially form part of the sample or knew others who would qualify to join the study. Once they had become familiar faces in these areas of San Antonio, the researchers began to speak with non-injecting heroin users, asking them to participate in the study, and asking them if they knew other people who would also join the study, effectively creating a snowball sample. In all, around 300 respondents were recruited to become part of the study.

This research shows that while a snowball sample is non-probability, it can be an effective way of recruiting a group of people who form part of a minority group or are part of the 'hidden population' for specialised research into a particular area.

Convenience sampling

A **convenience sample** is one that is drawn from a group of people or other sampling units that are 'to hand', sampling whoever is convenient to the researcher. An example of this that is often seen in everyday life is the researcher on the street with a clipboard. They simply ask anyone walking past if they want to participate in the research. True to its name, this type of sample is convenient to access, making recruitment quick and cheap.

Unsurprisingly, the major disadvantage of a convenience sample is its lack of representativeness. It is very likely that the sample obtained will be representative of the population of interest, particularly if you are interested in the population of a country, for example. Going back to the example of the researcher on the street with a clipboard, people walking down a particular street at a particular time on a particular day are not likely to represent the population as a whole.

Combining different sampling methods

Often, it's not as simple as choosing a single sampling method to deploy Many studies will use a combination of sampling methods in order to achieve a sample that fits the purpose of the study. In particular, different combinations of random sampling methods are common. For example, a study may start with a clustered sample, then stratify respondents within the cluster and draw a sample of individuals from within strata using systematic random sampling. This ensures a good spread of individuals who have different characteristics, but who are located within particular geographic areas to keep survey costs down.

From a non-probability perspective, a researcher may start with a convenience sample, then introduce quotas to ensure that certain groups of people are included in the study, and perhaps add an element of snowball sampling to achieve better representation of particular groups.

Over-sampling

Now that we have discussed different types of sampling methods in theory, we come to something slightly different – specifically, an explicit decision to over-sample people with particular characteristics. Over-sampling members of a particular group of individuals for inclusion in a study is a common technique that allows researchers to ensure that a) the population of interest can be reflected within a study, but also b) there are enough individuals from smaller groups to allow meaningful analysis.

An example of a longitudinal study which has over-sampled certain individuals to increase utility of the resultant data is the Millennium Cohort Study in the UK. The Millennium Cohort Study is a study of children born at the turn of the century in the UK, covering England, Scotland, Wales and Northern Ireland. If a simple random sample had been deployed, it would have been likely that the raw numbers of participants in Wales, Scotland and Northern Ireland wouldn't have allowed meaningful analysis of issues within those smaller nations. In addition to over-sampling in the smaller nations, children born in disadvantaged areas were over-sampled, as well as children with ethnic minority backgrounds. The resulting sample allows researchers to study the situation in the UK as a whole, but also facilitates a deeper look into the experiences of ethnic minority children, those growing up in deprived areas and those in devolved nations of the UK.

It is important for a user to longitudinal data to understand whether certain groups of people in the sample have been over-sampled. This is to ensure an understanding of who the sample reflects and whether the resultant analysis is a generalisation.

STUDY PROFILE

Millennium Cohort Study (MCS)

Established: 2000–2.

Country: UK.

Sampling unit: individuals.

Sample size at base: 18,818 individuals.

Frequency of interviews: irregularly: age 9 months and 3, 5, 7, 11, 14 and 17 years.

Participants: young people born between 2000 and 2002 in the UK.

Topics covered: physical, socioemotional, cognitive and behavioural development, behaviour and experiences, economic circumstances, parenting, relationships and family life.

Methods of data collection: face-to-face and online.

Innovative features: data linkage, cognitive assessments, DNA collection, anthropometrics.

Data availability: data are available to the research community via the UK Data Archive.

More information: https://cls.ucl.ac.uk/cls-studies/millennium-cohort-study/

WAS THE SAMPLE REFRESHED?

As we know, longitudinal studies follow the same people over time. One of the drawbacks of doing this is that respondents drop out of the study as time passes. This means that after a few waves of data collection, the sample who are still participating may look a little different from the sample that were included in the study when it started. This could mean that the sample is no longer representative.

In order to maintain representativeness of studies over time, sometimes refreshment samples are added. This is done to counter the fact that some people have dropped out. Additionally, refreshment samples might be added because the fact that participants' ages make the study less representative of the younger generations (in the event that the study aims to provide a representative sample of all adults in a country, for example). As well as increasing representativeness, refreshing a sample also increases the number of responses that are available for analysis. If a sample becomes too small, even if it is still representative of the population of interest, it may not be able to be used for certain types of analysis.

An example of a study that refreshes the sample regularly to ensure that it remains representative is the Nihon University Longitudinal Study of Aging (NUJLSOA). As the NUJLSOA aims to be representative of the population aged 65 and over in Japan, they need to keep adding participants as current study members age to ensure that those at the younger end of the spectrum continue to be represented in the study.

WAS THE SAMPLE BOOSTED?

A boost sample in a longitudinal study is similar to a refreshment sample in that additional participants are added to the study after it has already started. However, the aim of a boost sample is slightly different in that certain types or groups of people are added to increase the numbers of that group. This makes analysis on specific subgroups of the sample possible. For example, in a study that represents a whole country, there might be interest in doing research on the experiences of migrants. However, a longitudinal study representing the whole country may not have enough migrants in the original sample to carry out meaningful analysis. Alternatively, it may be that the population now contains a much higher proportion of migrants than when the study first began. In order to overcome these issues, the study may wish to add a boost sample of migrants to allow depth analysis to take place.

SAMPLING ERROR

The common pitfall to be aware of when thinking about what type of sample a study employed is sampling error. At its most basic, sampling error is the error that occurs in analysis caused by the sample being unrepresentative of the population from which it was taken – that is to say, the sample doesn't accurately reflect the population of interest. The only way to guarantee no sampling error is to measure every single person in the population of interest. The vast majority of the time, this is simply not possible and, as such, sampling error is something we need to be aware of and live with.

There are methods by which sampling error can be reduced through design choices at the sampling stage. Designing a robust sampling procedure will decrease the likelihood that biases are introduced due to sampling error. Using probability sampling methods, such as those described above, is one way of reducing the likelihood that sampling error will have a large impact on analysis and therefore conclusions. Randomly selecting members of a population makes it more likely that those sample members will represent the population as a whole. The same is true if a carefully designed cluster or stratified sample is deployed. At the other extreme, non-probability methods, such as convenience sampling, increase the likelihood of sampling error causing biases in analysis.

As a rule, the larger the sample, the more likely the sample members are, as a whole, to represent the population of interest. Therefore, longitudinal studies with large samples, drawn using probability methods, will likely have less sampling error than small studies.

Sampling error is difficult – if not impossible – to deal with at the analysis stage. As such, it is important for a researcher to scrutinise data prior to use to understand how the sample was drawn and the impact this may have on sampling error. Ultimately, a researcher needs to acknowledge and understand the potential for bias in the data that has been introduced by sampling error, and the resultant impact this may have on the generalisability of findings.

CONCLUSIONS

There are a number of different methods for creating a sample for a longitudinal study, including those that deploy probability methods and those that use non-probability methods. Each sample design comes with its own benefits and drawbacks, which must be understood to assess the quality of the sample. Overarching all of this is the idea of sampling error – if a sample is to be drawn, then it very likely contains sampling error. Fully understanding how a sample was created is key to assessing the likelihood of the presence of sampling error, and resultant bias in the data.

Key learning points

- Samples can either be probability or non-probability. Probability samples are where the likelihood of selection for each individual from the population into the sample is known. For non-probability samples, the likelihood of selection is not known.
- Probability samples:
  - Simple random sample: where each of the sampling units have an equal chance of being chosen; all sample members are chosen completely at random.
  - Clustered sample: population of interest is divided into different groups, called clusters, and then a sample of those groups is drawn. The aim is that each of the clusters are homogeneous, but within each cluster there is heterogeneity.
  - Stratified sample: the sample is divided into different groups, called strata, and then individuals within those groups are sampled. Strata are based on some common characteristics that are of interest to the research.
- Non-probability samples:
  - Quota sample: groups of interest are created based on characteristics, and then sample members are recruited if they fit within those groups of interest.

  - Snowball sample: created by finding a few people that are of interest, then asking those people if they know other people who also fit the group of interest.
  - Convenience sample: the sample is drawn from a group of people or other sampling units that are 'to hand' - sampling whoever is convenient.
- Samples can be boosted or refreshed to increase the representativeness, or to increase the presence of certain subgroups or minorities in the sample which are of interest to researchers.
- Sampling error is the error that occurs in analysis caused by the sample being unrepresentative of the population from which it was taken. This is unavoidable for any study that deploys any sampling method, but the impact of sampling error can be reduced by having a large sample size, carefully designing the sample using probability sampling methods.

Check your understanding

1. Why would we sample for a longitudinal study in the first place? Why don't we just follow all individuals in the population of interest?
2. Briefly describe the benefits of using a probability sampling method.
3. What are the drawbacks of using a non-probability sampling method?
4. What are the differences between a boost sample and a refreshment sample?
5. How can we reduce the likelihood of sampling error causing bias in our analysis?

WANT TO FIND OUT MORE?

The resources below are great sources of additional information on the content covered in this section.

An overview of survey sampling techniques:

Hibberts, M., Burke Johnson, R. and Hudson, K. (2012) 'Common survey sampling techniques', in Gideon, L. (ed.) *Handbook of Survey Methodology for the Social Sciences*. New York: Springer.

A summary of sample design issues in longitudinal surveys:

Smith, P., Lynn, P. and Elliot, D. (2009) 'Sample design for longitudinal surveys', in Lynn, P. (ed.) *Methodology of Longitudinal Surveys*. Chichester: John Wiley & Sons.

A history of survey sampling, alongside a focus on future directions:

Brick, J.M. (2011) 'The future of survey sampling', *Public Opinion Quarterly*, 75 (5): 872–88.

A discussion of refreshment samples in longitudinal studies:

Watson, N. and Lynn, P. (2021) 'Refreshment sampling for longitudinal surveys', in Lynn, P. (ed.) *Advances in Longitudinal Survey Methodology*. Hoboken, NJ: Wiley.

4

ATTRITION AND MISSING DATA

OVERVIEW OF CONTENT

This chapter discusses missing data in the content of longitudinal studies. The concept of attrition will be introduced, which is a type of missing data unique to longitudinal studies. The chapter will look at different types and patterns of missing data and explain the impact of missing data on analysis.

Two different approaches to dealing with missing data will be discussed – imputation and weighting – in order to minimise the impact of bias on analysis.

Learning outcomes

After you have read this chapter, you will be able to:

- describe what missing data is;
- describe attrition as a special type of missing data;
- explain how attrition and missing data can cause problems for the analysis of survey data;
- describe the different types of missing data and their potential impact on estimates;
- understand how imputation and weighting can be used to minimise the bias caused by missing data.

ATTRITION AND MISSING DATA

Attrition

Attrition can be considered one of the major methodological problems in longitudinal studies. At its most simple, attrition is where participants of a study drop out or, as it is also known, 'attrit'– in other words, they no longer take part in the study. Figure 4.1 shows what attrition may look like in a longitudinal study across three waves.

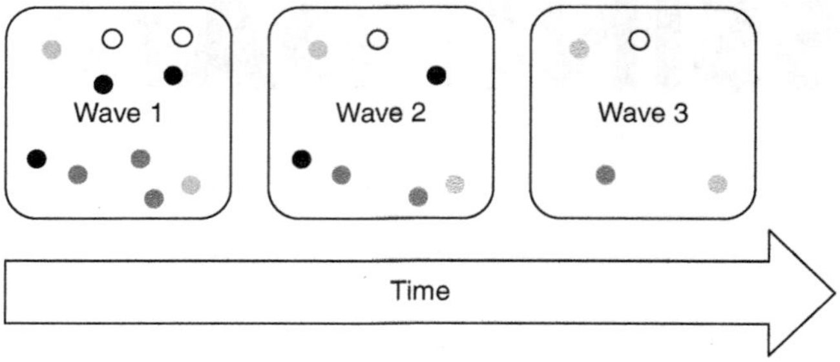

Figure 4.1 A visual representation of attrition

Given that the aim of a study is to follow people over time, this can cause problems. There are a few reasons why study members may attrit.

- *Attrition through refusal*: participants of a study may decide they do not want to take part any more. As such, they refuse to participate at future waves of a longitudinal study.
- *Attrition through loss to follow-up*: over time, participants in a longitudinal study are likely to move house or change their contact details. As a result, the study may be unable to locate them to invite them to participate in the next wave of the study. Alternatively, a study may simply not know whether the person has moved or not – they just can't get into contact with them. Either scenario causes attrition through loss to follow- up.
- *Attrition for other reasons*: if a study participant dies, they obviously will no longer be able to participate or, if they become seriously unwell, they may not be able to participate.

Attrition can be a big problem for a longitudinal study because usually it is not random – that is to say, those who decide not to take part in a study at some point are usually different in some way from those who remain in the study. The same is true of those who are 'lost' to the study – people who move house or are very difficult to contact may be different in some way to those who are not. As such, attrition can cause bias. Bias means that the results of a study may not be applicable to the population which the study intends to represent.

As a starting point, let's look at a real-world example of attrition. Young and colleagues analysed data collected by the Australian Longitudinal Study on Women's Health to look at the reasons for attrition and its predictors.

Research spotlight

Young, A.F., Powers, J.R. and Bell, S.L. (2006) 'Attrition in longitudinal studies: Who do you lose?'

The Australian Longitudinal Study on Women's Health started in 1996, recruiting three separate cohorts of women: those who were 'younger', 'mid-age' and 'older'. Each group was followed up regularly using mailed questionnaires, allowing an assessment of attrition over time of the different groups of women. Young and colleagues focused specifically on attrition between the first two waves of the study and came up with five categories of attrition: 1) death of the respondent; 2) illness of the respondent which prohibited further completion of surveys; 3) withdrawal of the respondent; 4) contact not made with the respondent; 5) non-completion of the questionnaire.

The first point to note is the overall completion rate of the second survey. In total, 68 per cent of the younger cohort completed the second survey, compared with 90 per cent of those classified as mid-age and 84 per cent of the older age group. Instantly, differences in attrition rates based on age can be seen. Extending this finding to a study of adults aged 16+ in a particular country, for example, demonstrates instantly how attrition could have an impact on sample representativeness and therefore a generalisation of findings - if around one third of younger participants attrit after the first wave and only one in ten middle-aged respondents do so, the sample at the second wave starts to look quite different from the original sample.

As well as the differential attrition by age, the reasons for attrition in each age group were also different. The main reason for attrition in the younger age group was that contact could not be made with the respondent, but for the older age group the reason was withdrawal.

In addition to looking at reasons for attrition, the authors also explored factors that predicted attrition - specifically, were there certain groups of people who were more likely to attrit than other groups? Across all age groups, they found that those from a non-English speaking background and those with lower levels of education were more likely to attrit. Additionally, respondents who smoked were more likely to attrit. For the mid-age and older cohorts, those who reported better health in the first survey were more likely to take part in the second survey.

The authors highlighted that a key reason for understanding attrition in longitudinal studies is to understand who at the first wave may need additional effort made with them in order to retain them in the study.

STUDY PROFILE

Australian Longitudinal Study on Women's Health

Established: 1995.

Country: Australia.

Sampling unit: individuals.

Sample size at base: over 58,000.

Frequency of interviews: dependent upon the cohort.

Participants: cohorts of women born in Australia in 1921-6, 1946-51, 1973-8 and 1989-94.

Topics covered: health, health behaviours, risk factors, use of health-related services, time use, family, workforce participation.

Methods of data collection: mail, online.

Data availability: data are available to the research community through a Data Access Application system.

More information: https://alswh.org.au/

The research by Young and colleagues highlights the point that those who attrit from a study are likely to be different from those who remain in a study, potentially causing bias in subsequent research done using the data. One of their interesting findings, which is particularly pertinent to a longitudinal study, is that the primary reason for attrition for the younger age group was the inability of the study team to contact respondents in that age group to invite them to participate. Basic and Rendtel explore this issue in more depth using the German Microcensus Panel to establish the impact of non-contact on subsequent bias.

Research spotlight

Basic, E. and Rendtel, U. (2007) 'Assessing the bias due to non-coverage of residential movers in the German Microcensus Panel: An evaluation using data from the Socio-Economic Panel'

The German Microcensus Panel is a longitudinal study collecting information on various aspects of the labour force. It has a rotating panel design whereby households are enrolled in the study for four years and then their participation ends; they are then replaced by a different household. However, people who move during the course of the study are not traced and not followed up at subsequent waves. Instead, people who move into the sampled address are included in the study instead (so actually the address is the sampling unit, not the family). This design gives researchers the opportunity to explore the impact of not tracing movers on the resultant data collected by the study.

Using comparable data from the German Socio-Economic Panel (SOEP), which does follow movers, the authors were able to assess the impact of the German Microcensus Panel design choice of not following residential movers on the estimates produced by the study.

They found that being a mover generally depends on changes in labour force status - for example, getting a (new) job, leaving a job, etc. - even when other demographic variables are accounted for. In turn, this means that the missing data that occurs as a result of not following up people who move house is not 'missing at random'. As such, movers are different in some way to non-movers and, by not following them, bias is introduced into the data.

What we have seen so far suggests that attrition can have an impact on the representativeness of data collected in a longitudinal study. This chapter goes on to explore different types of missing data and what we can do with data once it has been collected to minimise that impact.

STUDY PROFILE

German Microcensus Panel

Established: 1957.

Country: Germany.

Sampling unit: addresses.

Sample size at base: 1 per cent of the households in Germany.

Frequency of interviews: rotating panel, with households interviewed annually for four years.

Participants: people living in residential households in Germany.

Topics covered: households, family, labour market, migration, childbirths, housing conditions.

Methods of data collection: face-to-face, telephone.

Data availability: data are available to the research community for a fee through the Research Data Centres of the Federal Statistical Office.

More information: www.gesis.org/en/gml/microcensus

Other forms of missing data

Attrition is just one type of missing data in longitudinal studies, often referred to as '**monotone missing**'. This is where the respondent stops participating in a longitudinal study altogether. The other form of missingness is '**non-monotone missing**', where respondents in a longitudinal study drop out and then return to the study eventually. Therefore, the study has incomplete data on these individuals across time. Again, this type of missingness may not be random, causing a bias. Figure 4.2 shows different response patterns, categorising them into no missingness, attrition and non-monotone missing.

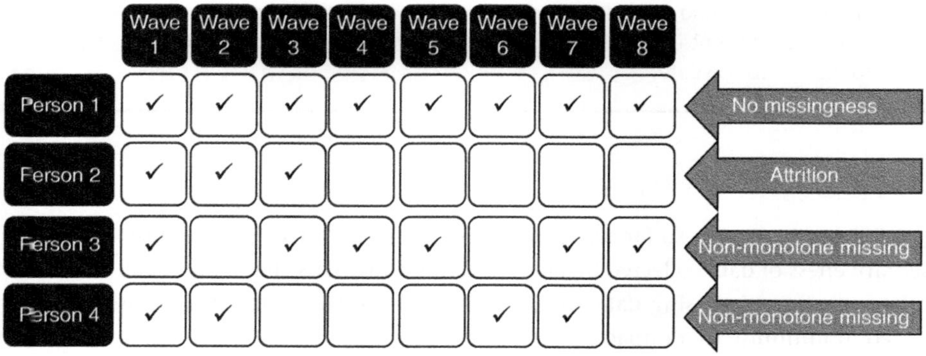

Figure 4.2 Response patterns showing no missingness, attrition and non-monotone missing

As well as missingness occurring for the entirety of a sampling unit (**unit non-response**) – for example, someone refusing to participate in an interview or being unable to do so – there also exists item missingness, or **item non-response**. Item non-response is where a respondent answers most of the questions in a questionnaire, for example, but does not provide answers for a few measures within the questionnaire. Both unit and item non-response are important to consider in term of analysis. The remainder of this chapter will look at the implications of missing data, types and patterns of missing data, and how to overcome this in analysis.

Implications of attrition and missing data

From an analytical view, there can be implications of using data from a longitudinal study where attrition or other forms of missingness have occurred (and realistically, this is the vast majority of longitudinal datasets that you will come across). A longitudinal study which has observations for every study member at every point in time is called a **balanced panel** (and, of course, a balanced panel can be created for any longitudinal study by dropping individuals from the sample who have not participated at every point in time). Conversely, where data are missing for certain participants at different timepoints, you have an **unbalanced panel**. The first thing to consider with an unbalanced panel is why the data are missing in the first place. Once you have understood this, there are steps you can take to correct or adjust it if necessary. A good starting point is to understand the different types of missingness and understand the implications of each. The section below outlines each of the types of missingness and the assumptions made about bias in relation to the missing data.

DIFFERENT TYPES OF MISSINGNESS

Missing Completely at Random (MCAR)

Data which is **Missing Completely at Random**, or MCAR for short, means that there is no difference between missing data and observed data (or at least for data which the researcher has access to) – that is to say, the missingness of the data hasn't caused any bias. An example of how this might happen could be postal questionnaires. Imagine that a representative group of people are asked to complete a paper questionnaire and then return it to the research team via the post, and all the people surveyed complete the questionnaire and put it in a post box. It is possible that some of those questionnaires then go missing in the postal system and never make their way back to the research team. The missing data caused by the lost questionnaires would be considered MCAR, because there is no systematic process that causes some data to be more likely to be missing. The missing data has occurred by chance, not because some people were more likely to fill the questionnaire in than others.

Cases where missing data are considered MCAR are the easiest to handle analytically. As no bias is introduced by the missingness, there isn't a need to adjust for this in any analysis conducted on the data, beyond excluding the missing values.

Missing at Random (MAR)

Missing at Random (or MAR) are data where the propensity for data to be missing has nothing to do with the variable or measurement you're interested in, but the missingness is systematically related to a different observed variable. To illustrate, it could be that you're interested in measuring the weight of a particular population. When you start this project, you might find that women are more likely to tell you their weight than men are. This causes missing data because many men have left that question blank. This doesn't necessarily cause a big problem for your analysis because most people are reporting their weight (whether it is high, low or somewhere in the middle), so you should get a good idea of the population's average weight overall.

However, you do know that the missingness in the data is not completely random because men are less likely to tell you their weight in the first place.

Handling data which are MAR is more complex than data which are MCAR, as adjustments may need to be made during the analysis stage to minimise any bias that may be introduced into the results through the missingness. The section below on 'dealing with missing data' introduces some methods that can be used to handle missing data.

Missing Not at Random (MNAR)

The other type of missing data is that considered **Missing Not at Random**, or MNAR (sometimes also known as Not Missing at Random, or NMAR). In cases where data cannot be considered MCAR or MAR, then it must be MNAR. Put simply, the value of the variable that is missing is related in some way to the reason it is missing. This can be illustrated by going back to our example of measuring the weight of a population. This time, though, imagine that instead of missing values of weight being related to the respondent's gender, the missingness is related to the respondent's weight itself. It could be that those with a particularly low weight are more likely to leave the question about weight blank, causing missing data. In this situation, the value of the missing data is related directly to the variable of interest. If we then use the MNAR data to get an average weight for the population surveyed, the value won't be accurate because there are a whole subset of missing responses which would change the average value if they were not missing.

Like data which are MAR, adjustments need to be made to the data during the analysis stage to ensure that bias is minimised as much as possible. The section below on 'dealing with missing data' covers some techniques that can be used to handle missing data.

DEALING WITH MISSING DATA

We have seen why missing data may occur in a longitudinal dataset and the problems that can occur as a result. Now we turn to what to do about missing data when it comes to a longitudinal dataset. There are a number of options:

- collecting missing data;
- complete case analysis;
- imputation;
- weighting.

Each of these are outlined in the subsections below.

Collecting missing data

In an ideal world, we would go back to respondents and try to collect all the data that are missing from the dataset. While this is often impractical (as it would likely add a lot of expense to a study) and perhaps not likely to be successful (given that there was probably a reason the respondent didn't provide the data in the first place), longitudinal studies can provide opportunities to do this for some variables.

Given that the nature of longitudinal studies is to return to respondents over time to collect more data, there is the option of reasking respondents to provide data that were missing at a previous sweep. This is possible for certain types of factual data, but less desirable in the case of attitudinal or, in some types, of behavioural data. For example, if a respondent did not provide their ethnicity at a particular sweep of data collection, the researcher could reasonably ask for this information again at a later time as it is unlikely that someone has changed their ethnic identity. Equally, it may be possible to ask a respondent to think back to what their job was previously in the event they didn't answer that question in the past. However, asking someone to recall what their political opinions or exercise habits were in the past is likely to be less fruitful or desirable (see Chapter 6 for an overview of recall and reporting, and some of the issues that may occur).

Ultimately, while this is possible for some variables, it is also something that has to be implemented by the study and clearly is not a viable technique for researchers to use at the analysis stage. As such, the following techniques are analytical, allowing researchers to deal with missing data once they have a dataset in front of them.

Complete case analysis

Complete case analysis is simply removing, or 'dropping', all cases for which complete data is not available in your analysis. This leaves a dataset in which every respondent has answers for every variable of interest at every time point.

While this may make analysis straightforward, as there's no need to do anything to account for missing data points, a large assumption is being made that may not be accurate. Doing complete case analysis assumes that those with all data for all variables of interest at every time point are representative of those who are missing some data – in other words, Missing Completely at Random. If this is not the case, and a different form of missingness is present in the data, removing respondents who do not have a complete set of data will introduce bias into the analysis.

For example, you might be interested in how personal income contributes to living arrangements over time. The longitudinal dataset you've chosen to use may have a considerable number of respondents who haven't answered the income question on a number of occasions (but they have at each sweep of the study told you what their living arrangements are). Complete case analysis would mean that you remove all respondents who haven't reported their income at every sweep of the study. However, it is possible that those respondents might be uncomfortable reporting their income because they consider it personal or sensitive information, particularly if it is much higher or lower than what they perceive to be 'average'. By removing these respondents, the picture you can build of how income affects living arrangements over time is likely to be biased, because those at the top and bottom ends of income are not included.

In addition, complete case analysis reduces the sample size available for analysis. Doing this can lead to reduced statistical power, meaning that an effect might be present if the data isn't visible.

Imputation

Put very simply, **imputation** is the process of replacing missing values with estimated ones. The estimations can be based on information known about the respondent already, from information known about the population of interest or from information from another case which shares similarities to the respondent with missing values. There are two forms of imputation (single and multiple) and within those a large number of specific methods that can be used to impute data. Imputation is most often used in the case of item non-response, but the theory can be expanded into unit non-response. In this section, we will first cover some of the main methods that can be used to impute data, and then discuss the pros and cons of using a single or multiple imputation strategy.

Mean imputation

Mean imputation is the process by which any missing values on a particular variable are replaced with the mean average of all the values that are available for that variable in the dataset. If the data for the variable for which you're using mean imputation is MCAR, this method is good because it preserves the sample mean, keeping the mean unbiased. Mean imputation is also often used because it is a quick and easy method to impute data and retain the sample size. However, there are significant drawbacks. Mean imputation does not preserve the relationships between variables. Given that the point of many research studies is rarely to calculate a population mean, and more likely to understand relationships between different variables, this imputation method is likely to bias results. Using mean imputation is likely either to show a stronger or a weaker relationship between two variables than actually exists. As such, it is usually considered a 'last resort' method of imputation in favour of some of the more sophisticated imputation methods discussed below.

As a slight side note, the median or the mode value of a particular variable can also be used to impute missing values rather than the mean. This works in the way described above, with the same benefits and drawbacks. As a reminder, mean, median and mode are all measures of central tendency or ways of finding the 'middle' of a set of data. The mean, often referred to as the average, is calculated by adding up all the numbers in the variable you're interested in, then dividing by the number of observations. The median is the middle number, calculated by ordering all the numbers of a variable you're interested in from the smallest to the largest, then taking the number that sits at the middle of the list. The mode is the most common number – simply the figure that appears most frequently in a variable of interest.

Hot-deck imputation

Hot-deck imputation is a method by which a value taken from a respondent in a dataset is used to fill a missing value for another respondent. The respondent who has a missing value and the 'donor' respondent should be similar, based on a number of observed characteristics that are available in the dataset for both respondents. The theory then follows that the imputed value is plausible, given the similarity of the donor and recipient respondents.

There are two main ways of selecting the donor respondent, with the donor respondent being the one that provides a value for the case that has a missing value. The donor can either be chosen randomly from a pool of respondents who all match the recipient to some degree. Alternatively, the donor can be chosen specifically, usually because they are the closest match to the recipient based on a number of observed characteristics.

Hot-deck methods of imputation tend to be popular as they are relatively easy to implement. Unlike some other methods, hot-deck imputation does not rely on model building to create imputed values, removing the risk of creating a model that is mis-specified (a mis-specified model being one that doesn't account for all the variables it should to give an accurate representation). Additionally, the imputed values are all plausible, given that they all come from observed values in the dataset, which is not necessarily true of some other imputation methods. Hot-deck imputation also allows the relationships between different variables to be retained, overcoming the issue discussed with mean imputation above.

However, as with all imputation methods, there are drawbacks and risks. With hot-deck imputation, there is a risk that imputed values all come from the same donor or a small pool of donor respondents. It is possible to set a limit on the number of times a single donor's value is used as an imputed value, but that may itself bring risks. The use of only a small pool of donors tends to be more likely with small datasets where there are a very limited number of similar respondents. As such, hot-deck imputation tends to be most successful when implemented on larger datasets with a big pool of donor respondents.

Regression imputation

Regression imputation is a form of imputation that relies on model building to provide values for missing data. This is a two-step process: 1) a regression model is built and run, based on the observed values for the variable that is to be imputed, plus a series of explanatory variables; 2) the model is then used to predict what the missing values on the variable of interest are. This process retains the relationships between different variables (a drawback of using mean imputation), although risks creating values that are implausible, given the reliance on a model rather than values observed elsewhere in the dataset.

There are two main forms of regression imputation: deterministic and stochastic. Deterministic regression imputation replaces missing values with the exact value that is predicted by the model that has been built. This often leads to imputed values that are too precise, as no random error is built into the model. Stochastic regression goes some way to overcoming this issue. Rather than replacing a missing value with the exact value predicted by the model, a random error term is added. This means that relationships between different variables are likely to be more accurate than when imputation is done using deterministic regression.

Readers who are less familiar with the intricacies of regression modelling need not be alarmed at this point; you don't need to know the technical details, but rather just the notion that imputation can be achieved via the construction of models. However, if you want to know more, there are further resources at the end of this chapter that expand on this topic.

Last observation carried forward

The 'last observation carried forward' method of imputation is one that is unique to longitudinal datasets. As the name suggests, if a variable is missing for a respondent at a particular sweep, it could be imputed using the last known value provided by that respondent at a sweep in the past. For example, this could work well for income. If a respondent has a missing value for a question on their income at a particular sweep, but provided the answer at a prior sweep, it is plausible to assume that carrying that past value into the present dataset is a reasonable estimate of their current income. While this is an assumption, of course, and their income may have changed for a variety of reasons, it is equally not an implausible value.

A very similar technique which is possible with a longitudinal study is 'next observation carried backwards'. Where a value is missing at one sweep, but a respondent provides that value at the next sweep, the more recently provided value can be copied into the matching variable from the previous sweep. The same assumptions apply as when you are using the last observation carried forward technique.

Single or multiple imputation?

Single imputation is a process by which missing values from a particular dataset are imputed and the complete dataset which results from this process is used for analysis. Each missing value is imputed with a single value, using any of the methods outlined above. One of the downsides of imputing missing values in a dataset is that generally the standard errors of statistics that are derived from imputed variables are too small.

If the standard errors are too small, then the p-value is also too small. This means that it is likely that a statistically significant result will be found where, in reality, it may not exist. This is true of all the imputation methods described in the section above. To overcome this problem, multiple imputation can be used.

Multiple imputation incorporates a level of uncertainty into the process of imputation, which increases the standard errors and provides a more robust and accurate estimation. In order to do this, instead of calculating a single value for each missing data point, multiple values are calculated, using a process that introduces a random error component to each value. Once this is done, you are left with multiple datasets, each with slightly different values for each of the missing data points. Each dataset is then analysed separately, giving slightly different estimates on the parameters of interest (because of the slightly different data in each dataset). The final step is to combine the results from all the analysis. Given the random error introduced into the process, the final result should be a reasonably unbiased estimate of all the parameters of interest.

Javanbakht and colleagues (2022) conducted an interesting test of single versus multiple imputation methods, which highlights the usefulness of each approach, depending on the data available and missingness.

Research spotlight

Javanbakht, M., Lin, J., Ragsdale, A., Kim, S., Siminski, S. and Gorbach, P. (2022) 'Comparing single and multiple imputation strategies for harmonizing substance use data across HIV-related cohort studies'

Using data from a cohort study of substance use and HIV, Javanbakht and colleagues set out to explore different strategies for imputing missing data. However, instead of starting with missing data, they created missing data from a complete dataset in order to test the effectiveness of different imputation strategies.

They looked specifically at self-reported substance use data, focusing on three drugs in particularly: heroin (as a low-prevalence drug), methamphetamine (medium-prevalence) and cannabis (high-prevalence). They set self-report data as missing for 10–50 per cent of each drug, and then conducted different types of single and multiple imputation to see which produced estimates that were the least biased – remember they were able to actually measure this because they knew what the complete dataset with no missingness looked like.

First, they used complete case analysis as a baseline – simply deleting all respondents for which data were missing and then conducting analysis. This produced biased estimates of substance use, particularly for heroin, where prevalence of use is particularly low.

The authors then moved on to using imputation. They found that for the high-prevalence drug (cannabis) where little data was missing, single imputation worked relatively well. However, multiple imputation produced the least biased estimates overall. They concluded that across a range of different conditions (different prevalence levels of drugs use and different levels of missing data), multiple imputation was the best performing approach for dealing with missing data.

Weighting

Weighting is another method by which missing data can be handled in a longitudinal dataset. In brief, a different 'importance' can be given to certain under-represented groups in a survey through the creation of weights. Weighting is particularly useful where missing data is caused by unit non-response or attrition. For a cross-sectional survey, weights are most often applied for two key reasons: 1) to account for unequal selection probabilities (often called a design weight); 2) to make sure that the people who participate in the survey reflect the population of interest on some key variables (often called a post-stratification weight). Of course, these things also apply to a longitudinal study. Let's start by taking these two types of weight in turn and then moving on to the longitudinal context.

Design weights

Unequal selection probabilities simply means that some people are more likely to be included in a survey than others. If this is true but analysis of the survey data doesn't reflect that, then bias could be introduced into results produced from the survey data. Unequal selection probabilities come about due to the design of the sample in the first place. It is rarely possible in a large-scale survey to ensure that everyone in the population of interest is equally as likely to take part. Let's look at how the Millennium Cohort Study in the UK designed their sample and how it resulted in unequal selection probabilities.

Research spotlight

Plewis, I. (2007) *The Millennium Cohort Study: Technical Report on Sampling* (4th edn)

The Millennium Cohort Study was designed to provide data about the generation of children born at the turn of the twentieth century in the UK, aiming to follow them as they grew up. The study aimed to be able to provide information about children as a whole, but also needed to contain enough children born into disadvantaged circumstances and from ethnic minorities in order to be able to report on issues specific to those groups too. In order to achieve those aims, a mix of sampling methods was used, combining random selection with stratification and clustering.

First, the sample was stratified by country - that is, England, Wales, Scotland and Northern Ireland. Then the population was further stratified by stratifying electoral wards (small geographical areas) using indicators for 'disadvantaged' (wards that fell into the top 25 per cent of the poorest wards based on the Child Poverty Index), 'advantaged' (wards that fell into the remaining 75 per cent of wards based on the Child Poverty Index, noting the term 'advantaged' in this context as a relative term), and, in England only, those wards with a high proportion of ethnic minority families. Within each strata, wards were organised based on geographic region and then size. Next, a certain number of wards were selected systematically within each strata (creating clusters). However, in order to get enough babies from disadvantaged backgrounds or from ethnic minorities, a larger proportion of wards with these characteristics were selected. Within each of the selected wards, all babies born within the target time frame were eligible to take part.

This immediately creates unequal selection probabilities. While the probability of selection of any one individual born in the right time frame was not zero - that is to say, everyone had some chance of being selected to participate - the chance was not equal for all babies born in the right time frame. By over-sampling wards with certain characteristics, some babies had a greater chance of being selected to take part than others.

However, the probability of an individual being selected to take part in the study was known and, as such, the study team were able to create design weights to account for unequal selection probabilities. Researchers were able to use these weights to ensure that bias caused by unequal selection probabilities was minimised in their analysis.

We have seen how the design of a sample for a study could introduce bias into data collected from that sample and how weights can be created to take this into account, reducing the bias. However, there is still likely to be some bias caused by the fact that not everybody in the sample chooses to take part, and in a longitudinal context this will differ across different waves of the study. Post-stratification weights are a method by which to attenuate this form of bias.

Post-stratification weights

The second reason to apply weights to a dataset is to make sure the responders to a survey reflect the population of interest. A simple example could be home versus international university students. Imagine that a survey is conducted that aims to understand the views of students at a university. When the survey results are compiled, the researchers find that 90 per cent of respondents are 'home' students – those who were living in the same country as the university before they started studying – and 10 per cent of respondents are international students. However, the registration information at the university shows that actually the student population is split between 80 per cent home students and 20 per cent international students. The survey data could be weighted to give slightly more importance to the responses of the international students in order that the results from subsequent analyses are more likely to reflect the views of the student population as a whole.

In practice, weights are often computed based on a variety of observed variables in a dataset rather than a single variable. Using external sources of data (such as population registry information or national estimates of population composition), researchers are able to estimate what the population of interest looks like across a number of key variables – for example, sex, age, ethnicity, employment status, income, and so on). The survey data can then be weighted to make sure that the data reflect the population of interest on those key variables.

Weighting in a longitudinal context

In a longitudinal context, there is an additional issue to address beyond the two discussed above. Specifically, there is an increasing number of patterns of response that are possible as the number of waves of a study increase. Individuals could take part in all waves of a study or all waves up until a certain point and then attrit, or they could take part in some waves, stop participating and then rejoin the study at a later date. Weights can be calculated to account for this varying participation for researchers to use when they are conducting analysis on a longitudinal dataset which requires data from multiple waves of the study.

The UK Household Longitudinal Study, also known as Understanding Society, is a good example of a longitudinal study that calculates weights to account for unequal selection probabilities and differential non-response in a longitudinal context. For more information on Understanding Society, see Chapter 1. The box below contains information about Understanding Society in terms of the weights that have been calculated and made available to researchers, to demonstrate the points made in this chapter about weighting, particularly in a longitudinal context.

Research spotlight

Understanding Society Main Survey User Guide (revision date: 29 October 2020)

Understanding Society produces datasets that are intended to be used with weights - specifically, weights to adjust for unequal selection probabilities, differential non-response and potential sampling error. As the User Guide points out, without using weights, the data user is making some large assumptions about the data. For example, the user would be assuming that estimated parameters of interest do not differ between different ethnic groups in the UK, those who have dropped out of the study and those who have not, and recent immigrants to the UK and those who have been living in the country for longer. In practice, it is highly likely that actually many estimates of interest would differ between these groups.

Understanding Society construct weights for analytical use that combine two different types of weights. First, there are design weights - those that account for the unequal probability of selection at the inception of the study. Second, non-response weights are created, accounting for the different levels of non-response (or attrition) at different waves of the study and also at different levels. Given that Understanding Society is a study that samples households and interviews all eligible people within those households, non-response weights are created at both the household level and the individual level. In combination, these weights create final weights that can (and should) be used when conducting analysis on the data.

The plural 'final weights' rather than 'final weight' in the previous paragraph was intentional. Given the complexity of the design of Understanding Society, the multiple respondents at each time point and the large number of waves of data collection, there are different weights appropriate for the intended analysis and the dataset on which that analysis is conducted. The Understanding Society User Guide provides guidance on how to select the appropriate weight for your intended analysis.

The other take-home here is that dataset user guides are key and should be considered your friend. Many longitudinal studies provide guides for researchers wishing to use their data which contain much of the detail about how the data should be used. These guides usually include descriptions of any weights available with the dataset, how they have been calculated and how they should be deployed. Researchers should consult available user guides before conducting analysis to ensure that they are aware of how best to treat the data.

CONCLUSIONS

Attrition is a phenomenon unique to longitudinal studies by virtue of their design and also one of the major methodological problems of such a study. Attrition tends to be a big problem for a longitudinal study because usually it is not random; those who decide not to take part in a study, or are unable to, are usually different in some way from those who do participate. As such, attrition can cause bias, which can then cause researchers to draw conclusions from research that may not accurately reflect what is actually happening in the population. Alongside attrition, missing data more generally is also problematic.

However, all is not lost. There are methods for accounting for attrition and missing data in a longitudinal dataset – namely, imputation and weighting. By assessing the missing data structure and pattern in a longitudinal dataset, study managers and researchers can make decisions about when and how to impute missing data, and implement weights to account for missingness to attenuate any negative effects it may cause.

Key learning points

- Attrition is a methodological problem unique to longitudinal studies. Put simply, it is where participants of a study drop out, or attrit. This can happen in different patterns - study members may stop participating completely or might participate in some waves of data collection and not others.

(Continued)

- Attrition and other forms of missing data, such as refusing to answer particular questions within a survey, is usually not random. Those who attrit or fail to provide responses to some questions are likely to be different in some way from those who provide all the data requested, leading to the occurrence of bias.
- There are three main forms of missing data in a survey context:
    - Missing Completely at Random (MCAR) - if data are MCAR, there is no difference between missing data and observed data and, as such, the missing data hasn't caused any bias.
    - Missing at Random (MAR) - data where the likelihood that data are missing has nothing to do with the measurement or variable of interest, but the missingness is systematically related to a different observed variable. In this form of missingness, some bias is introduced to the data.
    - Missing Not at Random (MNAR) - MNAR data are those where the value of the variable that is missing is related in some way to the reason it is missing. This is the most serious form of missingness, and if it is not accounted for explicitly in analysis, then results will be biased.
- There are a number of options for dealing with missing data. You could go back to a respondent and collect missing data, but this can be impractical and expensive. You could conduct a complete case analysis, where any respondents with missing values are dropped from the analysis. Alternatively, imputation or weighting could be used to attenuate bias.
- There are many alternative forms of imputation.
    - Mean imputation - any missing values on a particular variable are replaced with the mean of all the values that are available for that variable in the dataset.
    - Hot-deck imputation - a value is taken from a respondent in a dataset and used to fill a missing value for another respondent. The respondent who has a missing value and the 'donor' respondent should be similar, based on observed characteristics that are available in the dataset for both respondents.
    - Regression imputation - a regression model is built and run, based on the observed values for the variable that is to be imputed, plus a series of explanatory variables, then the model is used to predict what the missing values on the variable of interest are.
    - Last observation carried forward - an imputation method unique to longitudinal studies, whereby if a variable is missing for a respondent at a particular wave, it could be imputed using the last known value provided by that respondent at a past wave.
- Weights can be created to handle missing data in a longitudinal dataset. A weight that causes different 'importance' can be given to certain underrepresented groups in survey data analysis. Weights can be applied to account for unequal selection probabilities (often called a design weight), and to make sure that the people who participated in the survey reflect the population of interest on some key variables (often called a post-stratification weight). In the longitudinal context, weights also need to account for varying participation across waves.

Check your understanding

1. What might cause missing data in a longitudinal study?
2. Briefly describe the three types of missing data and indicate whether each type of missingness might cause problems for data analysis.
3. What are the benefits and drawbacks of conducting complete case analysis?
4. Briefly describe the main types of imputation: mean, hot-deck, regression and last observation carried forward.
5. What are the main reasons for using weights when analysing longitudinal survey data?

WANT TO FIND OUT MORE?

The resources below are great sources of additional information on the content covered in this section.

For more information on types of missing data (MCAR, MAR, MNAR) and how to handle missingness:

Bennett, D.A. (2001) 'How can I deal with missing data in my study?', *Australian and New Zealand Journal of Public Health*, 25 (5): 464–9.

For a discussion of attrition and how to handle missing data:

Twisk, J. and de Vente, W. (2002) 'Attrition in longitudinal studies: How to deal with missing data', *Journal of Clinical Epidemiology*, 55 (4): 329–37.

For information on imputation in a longitudinal context:

Spiess, M., Kleinke, K. and Reinecke, J. (2021) 'Proper multiple imputation of clustered or panel data', in Lynn, P. (ed.) *Advances in Longitudinal Survey Methodology*. Hoboken, NJ: Wiley.

For more information on weighting in a longitudinal context:

Lynn, P. and Watson, N. (2021) 'Issues in weighting for longitudinal surveys', in Lynn, P. (ed.) *Advances in Longitudinal Survey Methodology*. Hoboken, NJ: Wiley.

5

PANEL CONDITIONING

OVERVIEW OF CONTENT

This chapter introduces **panel conditioning**, a phenomenon unique to longitudinal studies. Put simply, panel conditioning is where an individual's response to a question at a particular point in time is influenced by a response they gave at a previous time point. The chapter will explore theories that try to explain the occurrence of panel conditioning, as well as how researchers can assess whether there is an impact of panel conditioning in a longitudinal dataset.

Learning outcomes

After you have read this chapter, you will be able to:

- explain what panel conditioning is;
- explain why panel conditioning can be a problem in longitudinal studies;
- understand some of the reasons why panel conditioning may occur;
- understand the methods for assessing panel conditioning in a longitudinal study.

WHAT IS PANEL CONDITIONING?

In the social sciences, the act of observing or measuring something can cause a change in the thing that is being measured if the subject of interest is aware that they are being observed or measured. This is a phenomenon that has been known for a long time and is often known as the **Hawthorne effect**.

Longitudinal studies present a scenario in which something akin to the Hawthorne effect can be seen in action. Asking the same set of people to answer the same questions over time can cause **panel conditioning**, where an individual's response to a question at a particular point in time is influenced by a response they gave previously – that is to say, they answer differently than they would if they were taking part in the survey for the first time. It might be that the response is the same as the one given previously or that the respondent changes their answer. Additionally, it could be that the quality of a response is improved (or worsened) as a result of panel conditioning.

In all cases, it could be that responses at both (or multiple) time points are accurate, or it could be that one or multiple responses are not accurate, leading to measurement error. This source of measurement error is unique to longitudinal studies.

What is measurement error? It is another type of error that may be present in longitudinal data or any other data, for that matter. We saw in Chapter 3 that sampling error can be introduced into a dataset at the point of choosing a sample to participate. Measurement error is a different form of error introduced at the measurement stage. Put simply, it is the difference between the measured value of something and the true value – an error introduced at the point of measurement of a value. Panel conditioning is a type of measurement error.

It should be noted at this point that there has been a lot of research into panel conditioning and the effects it may have on survey responses. Some of this research has found evidence for panel conditioning and some has found no evidence at all. This suggests that panel conditioning may occur under certain conditions in relation to certain topics or for certain respondents. There is no evidence to suggest that it occurs in a uniform or blanket way. However, given the potential impact it can have on longitudinal data, it is important to understand why it might occur and what can be done to assess the impact. Understanding the potential for measurement error allows researchers to critically assess a dataset before and during analysis.

Let's start with why panel conditioning might occur in the first place. There are a number of theories to explain why panel conditioning may occur, which are outlined in the section below.

WHY MIGHT PANEL CONDITIONING OCCUR?

Recall and length of time between waves

In the context of a longitudinal study, if a respondent is asked to answer the same question at various sweeps of a study, they may recall what they said at a previous interview. Some respondents may then choose to give the same answer again, even if their attitude or behaviour has changed. There is no consensus on why this might be the case (with theories ranging from the desire of a respondent to appear consistent in their answers, to respondents wanting to reduce the burden of the interview and therefore providing the same answer as before without having to expend the mental energy checking whether the real answer is the same or not), but it is important to note its occurrence.

The issue of recall in relation to panel conditioning leads to the question of whether there is an ideal length of time between waves of a longitudinal study. While there have been few empirical tests of the effect of different periods of time between waves of a longitudinal study and the subsequent impact on panel conditioning, it is generally thought that the larger the amount of time between the interviews, the less likely panel conditioning is to occur and respondents are less likely to remember the response they gave at a previous point in time – although, of course, this can lead to other issues with the accuracy of recalled information. See Chapter 6 for a summary of recall issues more generally.

Research by Zwane and colleagues does provide some empirical evidence that the closer the interviews are together, the more likely panel conditioning is to occur.

Research spotlight

Zwane, A.P. et al. (2011) 'Being surveyed can change later behavior and related parameter estimates'

Zwane and colleagues conducted several experimental studies that aimed to assess the extent to which being surveyed can affect subsequent behaviour and estimates of research interest, one of which also allowed an assessment of the impact of a short gap between surveys and a longer gap. Specifically, they looked at the impact of frequent (every two weeks) versus infrequent (every six months) surveys on the use of a water treatment product in Kenya and subsequent health outcomes. Participants were randomly assigned to either the frequent or infrequent survey group.

The findings suggest that those who were in the frequent survey group were more likely to have higher levels of the water treatment product detected in their water source and less likely to report health problems associated with poor quality drinking water in their child or children.

The authors concluded that the more frequent survey schedule biased the parameter estimate that was of interest in the first place in a way that the less frequent surveys did not, leading to the assessment that a larger gap between waves of a longitudinal study is preferable for unbiased estimates.

In addition to this empirical test of the effect of frequent versus infrequent survey follow-ups on the occurrence of panel conditioning, Warren and Halpern-Manners (2012) conclude that from their assessment of the existing literature, panel conditioning effects are more likely to occur when waves of a study have less than a month between them, and findings are more split when the follow-ups occur between a month and year after each other.

Learning and the practice effect

Longitudinal studies often involve complex questionnaires by the nature of the information they want to collect. As the point of longitudinal studies is to track individuals across the life-course and understand the sequence of life events experienced, questionnaires often look to capture details about anything that has changed since the last interview. This often leads to questions that trigger a set of follow-up questions when answered in a particular way. For example, we could think about the example of capturing information about the educational qualifications of respondents.

A study may ask respondents at every sweep whether they have gained any new qualifications since the last interview. Responding 'yes' to that question will often lead to a lengthy set of follow-up questions that capture the type of qualification, how long it took to complete, the grade achieved, details about the awarding body, and so on. Respondents may learn that if they say 'yes', they will get these additional questions, lengthening the interview. To avoid this, some respondents may answer incorrectly, failing to report that they have gained a new qualification and thus reducing the number of questions they will be asked, but introducing measurement error into the data.

However, there may also be a learning process, or practice effect, that works in the opposite direction, increasing the accuracy of responses given by longitudinal study members over time. As a result of asking respondents the same questions or asking them to complete the same tasks, multiple times across the life of the study, it may be the case that as a respondent becomes more familiar with the task they are expected to do – for example, answer survey questions thoroughly or complete a particular task such as a cognitive assessment – therefore the more likely their answers will be complete and accurate. This could be deemed a 'practice' effect. As with the other theories as to why panel conditioning may occur, changes in responses may be seen where really there is no change in behaviour or attitudes. In this case, the earlier data provided were less accurate or complete than the later data.

Increased awareness of a particular topic

It is possible that by asking about a topic repeatedly, a respondent may become more aware or informed of the issues around that particular topic. As a result, a change in behaviour or opinion may occur. A good example would be around political opinions and voting behaviour. If a respondent is often asked about whether they voted and who for, they may take time to reflect on the issue of voting and the political parties available for them to vote for. Subsequently, they may end up changing their behaviour by going out to vote where they wouldn't have done previously or voting for a different party.

The idea of asking about a topic in the context of a survey leading to behaviour change was demonstrated experimentally by Kraut and McConahay in 1973 in relation to voting behaviour.

Research spotlight

Kraut, R.E. and McConahay, J.B. (1973) 'How being interviewed affects voting: An experiment'

It was known by Kraut and McConahay in the 1970s and the wider research community at the time that the mere fact of being interviewed may have an impact on subsequent behaviour. However, at that time very little empirical research had been done to evidence and explore this effect. The authors set out to investigate whether conducting an interview with members of the public in a particular geographical area about voting preferences and behaviours would lead to subsequent behaviour changes in upcoming elections.

The study was experimental in design, whereby a pool of participants was selected and then randomly allocated to one of two groups. One group would be interviewed prior to the elections and one would not be interviewed at all (acting as a control group to demonstrate what would happen in the absence of an interview).

The findings strongly indicate an effect of the interview on subsequent turnout - those who were interviewed about political topics prior to the election were twice as likely to vote than those who were not interviewed. Furthermore, the turnout rate among those who were not interviewed was not significantly different from the turnout rate for the area as a whole, adding weight to the conclusion that it was the interview that affected the turnout rate for that group, rather than something to do with the specific participants chosen.

This demonstrates that even a single interview can have a relatively large impact on behaviour in the 'real world', reminding us that in a longitudinal study context, we should be aware of the potential impacts of multiple interviews on the data collected - in other words, panel conditioning.

Subsequent to the research by Kraut and McConahay on voter turnout, there has been a wealth of work to demonstrate the theory that interviewing people about particular topics can change behaviours and attitudes. This has covered many different topic domains, including couple satisfaction, student behaviour in universities, health behaviours, and many others.

An extension of this theory, or perhaps a particular facet, relates in particular to attitudes. It goes that asking respondents about their attitudes to particular things repeatedly during the course of a longitudinal study may encourage respondents to form attitudes where perhaps they hadn't had them before or rethink or crystallise existing attitudes. Therefore, panel conditioning may be particularly at play in cases where individuals do not have fully crystallised opinions on particular topics.

Reduction in social desirability bias

Social desirability bias refers to the phenomenon of a survey respondent failing to answer a question accurately if they believe their answer is not a socially desirable thing to say. Rather than giving the embarrassing or undesirable answer, they give an answer which they believe is socially desirable. As longitudinal studies visit people multiple times, the study may build up a level of rapport or trust with their participants. As respondents become more familiar with, or trusting of, the study they are participating in, it may be that they feel more comfortable revealing behaviours and attitudes that are not socially desirable. Previously, a respondent might have given a socially desirable answer to an interviewer as they didn't want to reveal a behaviour or attitude they felt would not be acceptable, but as time goes on and they become more trusting of the study, they might start to give responses that are accurate but are not socially desirable. As such, a change in behaviour or attitude will be seen where in reality no change has occurred – it's simply that previous behaviours or attitudes were misreported. This could be one of the reasons for the occurrence of panel conditioning.

Alternatively, it may not be trust of the study itself per se, but rather increased trust in the specific interviewer that can cause reduced levels of socially desirable responding. Often longitudinal studies try to have the same interviewers visit the same study members over time in a bid to increase rapport between interviewer and interviewee, and improve response rates and data quality. A study by Kühne (2018) demonstrates interviewer continuity and reduced social desirability bias playing out in a longitudinal study in Germany.

Research spotlight

Kühne, S. (2018) 'From strangers to acquaintances? Interviewer continuity and socially desirable responses in panel surveys'

Kühne set out to explore the impact that interviewer continuity in the context of a longitudinal study would have on responses given by participants. Using the theory outlined above, he suspected that by one interviewer conducting multiple follow-up interviews with a longitudinal study respondent, increased rapport and trust would be established between interviewer and interviewee, leading to reduced levels of socially desirable responding.

Data from the Socio-Economic Panel Study (SOEP) in Germany was well placed to explore this research question. The survey is predominantly conducted face-to-face and the study team try to ensure interviewer continuity as much as possible. By 2014, the average respondent had had the same interviewer for around five years, although some have known their interviewer for 30 years or more.

Looking at socially desirable responding, Kühne found increased socially desirable responses for respondents who had experienced an interviewer change. On the other hand, respondents who were interviewed by the same interviewer more than once were less likely to choose a socially desirable response after the first interview with that interviewer implying that as familiarity with an interviewer grows, so does trust, leading to more honest responding.

STUDY **PROFILE**

Socio-Economic Panel Study (SOEP)

Established: 1984.

Country: Germany.

Sampling unit: households.

Sample size at base: c. 15,000 households.

Frequency of interviews: annually.

Participants: individuals aged 12+ resident in sample households.

Topics covered: household composition, occupational biographies, employment, earnings, health and satisfaction indicators.

Methods of data collection: face-to-face interviews, mail questionnaires.

Innovative features: refugee boost.

Data availability: data are available to the research community via the SOEP Research Data Center.

More information: www.diw.de/en/diw_01.c.678568.en/research_data_center_soep.html

Increased trust in the study

Related to the previous point on social desirability bias, a more general process may be occurring in terms of trust in the study. As respondents in a longitudinal study become familiar with the study process, understand its importance and trust the study to look after the information they give, they may be more likely to answer more honestly and accurately. This seems particularly true for topics that may be considered by respondents to be more sensitive. An example to illustrate this could be income. Some respondents find questions that ask about their sources and level of income intrusive and quite sensitive. As such, they may refuse to answer those questions in a survey or edit their response to avoid giving the true or accurate figures. However, as trust in the study increases over time, some respondents may become more comfortable answering those questions accurately.

Fisher (2019) looked at the example of income in the UK Household Longitudinal Study, also known as Understanding Society (see Chapter 1 for an overview of Understanding Society), to explore whether panel conditioning could be observed in the study on the questions pertaining to income in particular.

Research spotlight

Fisher, P. (2019) 'Does repeated measurement improve income data quality?'

Fisher was interested in the quality of income data provided by respondents in the longitudinal context, investigating whether measurement of income improves over time. He exploited a natural experiment in the UK Household Longitudinal Study in order to answer this question.

Fisher identified two reasons why the measurement quality of income data may improve over time. First, panel conditioning, and second, dependent interviewing, a technique where responses from a previous survey are 'fed forward' into the next survey, to remind respondents of what they reported previously. See Chapter 6 for more information on dependent interviewing.

The design of Understanding Society allowed these two effects to be separated out. First, the periods over which respondents are interviewed for each wave overlap, which means that some respondents are interviewed in the same calendar year but in different study waves. Second, the dependent interviewing used means that respondents are asked to provide a response to a question and then are prompted by what they said to the same question at the previous wave and are able to change their initial response. However, both the initial and second response are recorded. For the income questions, this type of dependent interviewing was used for the questions that ask about types of social benefits (welfare) received, allowing researchers to assess which benefits each respondent would have failed to report without the use of dependent interviewing. Taken together, the effects of panel conditioning and dependent interviewing separately on income data quality can be assessed.

Fisher found that being interviewed for a second time increased mean income by 8 per cent compared with the first interview. This is driven primarily by unearned income, such as pensions and benefits. One third of that effect can be explained by dependent interviewing, with the remaining two thirds due to panel conditioning effects. There is also evidence to suggest that some of this change is due to improved reporting, suggesting higher data quality in later waves for the income questions.

Fisher's research demonstrates how panel conditioning can be a positive thing for a longitudinal study, through improved data quality. However, it also highlights that panel conditioning can lead to variable data quality across waves, making direct comparisons from wave to wave more complex.

Summary

In practice, it is likely that a longitudinal study will experience more than one of these forms of panel conditioning over time. The literature in the area of panel conditioning also highlights that more needs to be done to determine whether panel conditioning is more likely to occur for particular topics, in studies with different design features or for respondents with particular characteristics.

ASSESSING PANEL CONDITIONING

Very often, researchers looking at longitudinal data assume that any change or stability seen in individual responses over time is true change or stability. However, as we have seen earlier in this chapter, that may not necessarily be the case. As a result, it is useful to understand how to assess and control for panel conditioning.

Panel conditioning is notoriously hard to control because it is very difficult to isolate from other factors – that is to say, there could be a confounding factor. A confounder is something that may influence the apparent relationship seen between two variables, meaning that the relationship is actually spurious or, in other words, there isn't actually a cause-and-effect relationship. In the case of panel conditioning, confounders may include true attitude or behaviour change, change in the mode of administration of the questionnaire (see Chapters 8 and 9 for more information on data collection mode) or changes in the wording or layout of the question itself (see Chapter 7 for a summary of this issue), all of which can change responses independent of panel conditioning.

Despite these confounders and complexities, a number of approaches that could be used to assess the magnitude of panel conditioning have been proposed. The following sections will explain three of these approaches.

Looking at change over time among a single group

A number of studies simply look at changes in responses over time among a group of respondents participating in a longitudinal study. By looking at particular response patterns, one may be able to tell if panel conditioning appears to be at play. For example, by noting a reduction in the proportion of respondents offering 'no opinion' responses as they respond to more and more waves of a panel, you may be able to conclude that panel conditioning is at play.

However, given that there is no comparison group, it is difficult, if not impossible, to disentangle panel conditioning from what may be genuine attitude change among participants. As such, the two methods discussed below may be a better way of removing the confounder of true change over time from panel conditioning effects.

Baseline, then follow-up comparison

A second approach for assessing panel conditioning is experimental in nature and uses a treatment group who receive a baseline survey and then a follow-up survey at some point later, and a control group who receive only the follow-up survey. If the control group are not significantly different on any key demographics or other characteristics from the treatment group, then a comparison of responses between the two groups to the follow-up survey can allow for an assessment of the magnitude of panel conditioning effects.

While this method is great for researchers for assessing panel conditioning under different circumstances, it is less useful for designers and users of longitudinal studies already in field. However, the third method, described below, can be used to explore panel conditioning in existing longitudinal studies.

Comparing longitudinal and 'fresh' responses

For existing longitudinal studies that want to assess the impact of panel conditioning on their respondents, or researchers who are interested in doing so, a comparison can be made between responses to a longitudinal study with responses from a 'fresh' group drawn from the same population. In short, the 'fresh' respondents would receive the same questions as the longitudinal respondents had in a particular wave of a study, and the differences between those responses were compared, the theory being that if the two groups were both representative of the population of interest, any difference would be down to panel conditioning.

However, the drawback here is that the longitudinal study may have suffered some non-random attrition, and so the comparison between the fresh and longitudinal sample may be confounded with attrition.

An extension of the comparison of longitudinal and 'fresh' responses to assess panel conditioning is a rotating panel design. A rotating panel design is one whereby respondents of a longitudinal study enter the study and participant for a certain number of waves before being replaced by fresh respondents. The refreshment usually occurs at every wave of the study, with a certain proportion of respondents leaving and joining the study. This means that at every wave, there are some fresh respondents and some who have already participated in one or more previous waves of the study.

Halpern-Manner et al. (2017) looked at whether they could find evidence of panel conditioning in the General Social Survey in the US, utilising its rotating panel design to do so.

Research spotlight

Halpern-Manners, A., Warren, J.R. and Torche, F. (2017) 'Panel conditioning in the general social survey'

Using the General Social Survey (GSS) in the US, Halpern-Manners and colleagues set out to investigate whether they could find evidence of panel conditioning and, if present the magnitude of the effects. The GSS is a longitudinal study with a rotating panel design, with members of the study invited to take part in three interviews. Each of the interviews has a core set of questions that are asked of respondents every time they participate.

In order to assess panel conditioning, the researchers used data from 2006, 2008 and 2010, and included in their sample everyone who had participated in at least two waves of data collection. This meant that half of their analytical sample entered the GSS in 2006 and half entered in 2008. A comparison was then made of the responses to the 2008 data, between the group for which 2008 was their first time participating and the group for which 2008 was their second wave of the GSS.

This comparison is sensible in a few ways. Any difference seen in responses when comparing a representative sample for whom 2008 was their first wave with those for whom it was their second wave should be down to panel conditioning. Given that the measurement occurred at the same time point, external factors, such as economic issues and political issues, were equal for respondents, removing a confounding layer. Additionally, only including those who responded to at least two waves of data collection meant that these respondents all have the same propensity to respond to the GSS more than once, potentially removing any bias that may result from attrition rather than panel conditioning.

So, what did Halpern-Manners and colleagues find? Testing the differences between the two groups showed that some respondents were prone to panel conditioning for some of the questions tested. In particular, those who had participated in the GSS previously were more likely to give less socially desirable answers to some questions on more 'controversial issues', such as sex before marriage and hateful speeches in public. They were also more likely to report more people living in their household, more generations living in their household and more visitors to their household, as well as being more willing to report their personal income. These differences are perhaps a result of increased trust with the study and therefore being more willing to 'open up' about their circumstances.

However, it should be noted that panel conditioning effects were not found for all questions studied, again flagging that the phenomenon seems to occur only in some situations and for some question topics.

STUDY **PROFILE**

General Social Survey

Established: 1972.

Country: United States.

Sampling unit: individuals.

Sample size at base: 1,500 target.

Frequency of interviews: almost annually until 1994, then every two years. In 2006, a rotating panel design was introduced, with each participant included three times.

Participants: adults aged 18+ resident in the United States.

Topics covered: civil liberties, crime and violence, intergroup tolerance, morality, national spending priorities, psychological well-being, social mobility, stress and traumatic events.

(Continued)

Methods of data collection: face-to-face, telephone.

Data availability: data are available to the research community through NORC at the University of Chicago.

More information: https://gss.norc.org/

Summary

The existence of panel conditioning in a longitudinal study can be assessed using a number of different methods. Some of these methods allow for exploration of the conditions and contexts under which panel conditioning may occur, and others allow researchers to assess its occurrence in a study that has already collected data.

CONCLUSIONS

We have seen in this chapter that panel conditioning can be a problem for a longitudinal study. Panel conditioning is a phenomenon unique to longitudinal studies whereby an individual's response to a question at a particular point in time is influenced by a response they gave at a previous time point – that is to say, they answer differently than they would if they were taking part in the survey for the first time.

There are a number of theories to explain why panel conditioning may occur, but the evidence is not conclusive. It is likely that panel conditioning affects different studies in different ways by virtue of their design and the topics they ask about, and also that some individuals may be more prone to panel conditioning than others.

However, there are methods that make it possible to assess whether panel conditioning is likely to have occurred in a longitudinal study, and also experimental designs that allow researchers to test its occurrence in different situations which add to the body of knowledge about the topic.

Key learning points

- Asking the same set of people to answer the same questions over time can cause something called panel conditioning. This is where an individual's response to a question at a particular point in time is influenced by a response they gave at a previous time point - that is to say, they answer differently than they would if they were taking part in the survey for the first time.
- There are a number of theories to explain why panel conditioning may occur:
    - Recall and length of time between waves. In the context of a longitudinal study, if a respondent is asked to answer the same question at various sweeps of a study, they may recall what they said at a previous interview, which then influences

what they report. Panel conditioning effects are more likely to be seen when waves of a study have a shorter gap between them than when the gaps between waves are longer.

- Increased awareness. It is possible that by asking about a topic repeatedly, a respondent may become more aware or informed of the issues around that particular topic. As a result, a change in behaviour or opinion may occur.
- Reduction in social desirability bias. As longitudinal studies visit people multiple times, the study may build up a level of rapport or trust with their participants. As respondents become more familiar with, or trusting of, the study they are participating in, it may be that they feel more comfortable revealing behaviours and attitudes that are not socially desirable.
- Increased trust in the study. As respondents in a longitudinal study become familiar with the study process, understand its importance and trust the study to look after the information they give, they may be more likely to answer more honestly and accurately. This seems particularly true for topics that may be considered by respondents to be more sensitive.

- The existence of panel conditioning can be tested for and assessed in a number of ways.
    - Looking at change over time among a single group. By looking at particular response patterns, one may be able to tell if panel conditioning appears to be at play. However, given there is no comparison group, it is difficult, if not impossible, to disentangle panel conditioning from what may be a genuine attitude change among participants.
    - Baseline, then follow-up comparison. By comparing a treatment group who receive a baseline survey and then a follow-up survey at some point later and a control group who receive only the follow-up survey, any differences in responses between the two groups to the follow-up survey can allow for an assessment of the magnitude of panel conditioning effects.
    - Comparing longitudinal and 'fresh' responses. A comparison can be made between responses to a longitudinal study with responses from a 'fresh' group drawn from the same population, with any difference between groups being due to panel conditioning. A rotating panel design is a good way of doing this in practice.

Check your understanding

1. What is panel conditioning and why can it be a problem for a longitudinal study?
2. Briefly describe why social desirability bias can have an impact on panel conditioning.
3. What are the learning and practice effects in relation to panel conditioning?
4. How can we assess the occurrence of panel conditioning in a longitudinal study?

WANT TO FIND OUT MORE?

The resources below are great sources of additional information on the content covered in this section.

For a summary of the evidence to date on panel conditioning:

Struminskaya, B. and Bosnjak, M. (2021) 'Panel conditioning: Types, causes, and empirical evidence of what we know so far', in Lynn, P. (ed.) *Advances in Longitudinal Survey Methodology*. Hoboken, NJ: Wiley.

For information on the psychology behind panel conditioning:

Sturgis, P., Allum, N. and Brunton-Smith, I. (2009) 'Attitudes over time: The psychology of panel conditioning', in Lynn, P. (ed.) *Methodology of Longitudinal Surveys*. Chichester: John Wiley & Sons.

6

RESPONDENT RECALL AND REPORTING

OVERVIEW OF CONTENT

This chapter will explore issues with respondent recall and reporting. A common approach in longitudinal studies is to ask respondents to recall events and experiences since their last interview, given that the desire to understand changes over time. However, this may introduce bias into data as recall can often be inaccurate. We will explore some of the different types of recall problems and theories behind why they occur. We will then go on to look at how study design can minimise the risk of recall problems occurring.

Learning outcomes

After you have read this chapter, you will be able to:

- understand what recall issues are;
- understand why recall issues can cause problems for longitudinal studies;
- describe some of the types of recall problems that exist in relation to longitudinal studies and the theories that try to explain their occurrence;
- understand how a longitudinal study can be designed to minimise the impact of recall issues on responses.

WHAT IS RECALL?

As longitudinal studies tend to be primarily interested in change over time, and how past events and experiences shape future outcomes, it is common for respondents to be asked to recall events since their previous interview. Specifically, participants might be asked to remember frequencies with which something occurred, dates when something happened or how long something lasted. For example, a participant may be asked whether they have moved home and when, any health problems they have experienced and how long they lasted, how many times they have visited a hospital as a patient, or changes in employment or income. Additionally, if participants are recruited initially as adults into a longitudinal study, they may be asked to provide details about their past to build up a picture of their life to date. This richness of data about life events over time and the specific time periods in which different things happened helps make longitudinal studies crucial to understanding the life-course.

However, the human memory is not perfect. There are many different reasons why recall can be imperfect, but the ultimate problem for a longitudinal study is that inaccurate recall can cause biases in the data collected. As we have already seen, bias can be a problem for accurate and representative data.

Before we get into the detail of the types of recall problem that may exist, let's look at research by Beckett et al. (2001). They explored the Malaysian Family Life Surveys, which offers an opportunity to examine some key questions in relation to recall and how it operates in a survey setting.

Research spotlight

Beckett, M., DaVanzo, J., Sastry, N., Panis, C. and Peterson, C. (2001) 'The quality of retrospective data: An examination of long term recall in a developing country'[1]

The Malaysian Family Life Surveys (MFLS) are a pair of surveys conducted around 12 years apart in Malaysia, the first wave in 1976-7 and the second in 1988-9. The sample for the first survey consisted of 1,262 households containing an ever-married woman, and the second survey followed up those households, along with a sample of now adult children from the first survey, alongside two new samples.

Each of the two surveys collected retrospective histories from respondents across a range of different topics. The sample who completed both surveys offer an opportunity for researchers to compare responses to both sets of histories, allowing an assessment of difference between the two sets of reports (which should, theoretically, be the same). Specifically, comparing responses to the same questions at two time points allows assessment of the impact of increased recall time on response.

Using Kappa coefficients (and subsequent interpretation using Landis and Koch's (1977) criteria), the authors found reasonable agreement between individual reports at the two time points. Agreement was substantial for whether the respondent's children were breast-fed, moderate for marital status and fair for whether the woman in the household ever worked, and for whether contraceptives were used. However, for events for which details were asked about, such as the number of months over which something occurred or the exact weight of a child at birth, agreement between the reports at the two points in time was lower. Beckett and colleagues also found that for events that happened further back in time, details were more likely to be forgotten, suggesting a recall issue associated with time - the further back something occurred, the more likely the memory is to be forgotten, blurred or inaccurate.

Event salience appears to be important also in predicting whether or not something is reported or forgotten. Events that the researchers believed to be less salient (important) for the respondent were more likely to be forgotten over time or at least not reported. The example used is house moves - moves that lasted short amounts of time were less likely to be reported in the second wave of the study than house moves that lasted for longer periods.

In sum, the study shows that as the recall period becomes longer, the data provided by respondents deteriorates in quality - either events fail to be reported at all or the details around those events are less accurate or not recalled. Additionally, event salience is important to recall; the more salient the event, the more likely it is to be recalled and with greater detail and accuracy.

Now that we have seen an example of recall in action in a longitudinal study and some of the apparent problems, let's turn to the detail of the recall problems that may exist in the longitudinal context.

STUDY **PROFILE**

Malaysian Family Life Surveys

Established: 1976.

Country: Malaysia.

Sampling unit: households.

Sample size at base: 1,262 households.

Frequency of interviews: two-wave study, 1976-7 and 1988-9.

Participants: households containing an ever-married woman (wave 1).

Topics covered: family structure, fertility, economic status, education/training, transfers, migration.

Methods of data collection: face-to-face.

Data availability: available from the RAND website.

More information: www.rand.org/well-being/social-and-behavioral-policy/data/FLS/MFLS.html

TYPES OF RECALL PROBLEMS

As already alluded to, there are a number of different types of recall problems or reasons why recall may be inaccurate. The section below outlines the major types of recall problems that might be experienced by a longitudinal study.

Telescoping

A particular type of recall problem is '**telescoping**', where respondents can perceive recent events as happening longer ago than they actually did (backward telescoping) and events from a long time ago happening more recently than they did (forward telescoping).

Why might this occur? There are many theories that try to explain the occurrence of telescoping, three of which I will outline below. The 'why' may not seem important for longitudinal studies, but, if you will bear with me, you will see that understanding why may help us to make informed longitudinal study design choices. It should be noted that the theories below are theories; there is no consensus view on whether one of them is ultimately 'correct'. Nevertheless, an understanding of them is useful.

The first theory discussed here is called the 'accessibility principle', developed by Brown and colleagues in 1985. The theory surmises that when people are asked to recall the date that things occurred, people estimate what the date was based on the level of detail they recall about an event. The implicit assumption then made is that if you remember a lot of detail about the event, you will assume that it was a recent event, whereas events with vague detail recall are likely to be assumed to be further in the past. However, for some people and some events, great detail will be remembered even though the event took place a long time ago, which leads to forward telescoping – reporting that the event happened more recently than it actually did. Brown and his colleagues illustrated this using the examples of two assassination attempts – those of Ronald Reagan and Pope John Paul II (among many others, but for simplicity these examples are highlighted). They asked respondents to record the date they thought the attempted assassination of each man took place. The majority of people thought that the attempt on Pope John Paul II's life took place in an earlier time period than that of the attempt on Ronald Reagan's life. In fact, these events took place the other way around. The authors argue that the assassination attempt on Ronal Reagan was far more heavily publicised and the details therefore are clearer in people's memories than that of the attempt on Pope John Paul II's life. As such, people are more likely to believe that the attempted assassination of Ronald Reagan occurred more recently than it did.

The next theory discussed here around why telescoping may occur in human recall is the boundary model, proposed by Rubin and Baddeley (1989). They suggest that telescoping occurs due to the way that people are often asked to recall events, specifically using bounded time periods. For example, a survey may ask a respondent to recall hospital visits that have occurred in the last year. It has been argued that events outside of the boundary may get 'forwarded' into the bounded period and reported on, creating a forward telescoping effect, where events are reported as happening more recently than they did. It should be noted, however, that while there are a number of studies that seem to show telescoping effects due to the boundary model, there is counter-evidence to suggest that it may not apply in all contexts.

The final theory of telescoping occurrence to be covered here is the associative model put forward by Kemp (1999). The theory posits that if someone is asked to recall an event for which they do not know the date, they use associated or the most similar information they are able to achieve to estimate a date. It is likely that the event for which they are able to retrieve information is more recent in time than the event with forgotten details (as memory generally tends to deteriorate over time) and as such a forward telescoping effect occurs.

In brief, understanding the telescoping effect and why it might occur could help guide us in longitudinal study design choices, such as the time periods over which we ask people to recall events, but also in understanding the bias that may be introduced into longitudinal data due to telescoping.

Omissions

Another problem with respondent recall is omissions, where an event is not reported at all. There seem to be two explanations for an omission: either an event that should be reported is simply forgotten by the respondent or the respondent explicitly chooses not to report it, despite knowing that the event should be reported to answer the question fully.

In terms of the first explanation for an omission – forgetting – there is evidence to suggest that events of low salience to the respondent are more likely to be forgotten than highly salient events, which ties into some of the theories of telescoping described above, as well as Beckett et al.'s (2001) research which we have discussed previously in this chapter. In addition, human memory tends to deteriorate over time, so asking respondents to recall events from a long time ago, particularly ones of low salience, may result in an accidental omission.

Intentional omissions, on the other hand, may be related to social desirability bias. In brief, social desirability bias is the tendency of some respondents to answer a question in a way they think is socially acceptable or desirable, despite the fact the response they give isn't accurate. In the context of omissions, this can lead to a respondent failing to report an event despite the fact that it happened. For more information on social desirability bias, see Chapter 5.

Commissions

The opposite recall problem to omissions is commissions. Rather than failing to report something that did occur, respondents may recall and report something that did not actually occur. While considered to be less common than errors of omission, it is still a mechanism by which data can be biased through a recall issue.

For some respondents, again, social desirability bias can be at play, as with omissions. However, instead of failing to report an undesirable event, a respondent may report an event perceived as desirable or inflate an estimate of the frequency of a socially desirable event happening, resulting in an error of commission and therefore potentially a biased estimate.

Reference period misinterpretation

One method often used to help respondents accurately recall historical information is the use of a reference period. For example, respondents may be asked to report how many visits they had made to a doctor over the last month or last year. In the context of longitudinal surveys in particular, reference periods are often used to assess what has happened to the respondent since the last interview took place – so the reference period in this case would be set up as 'since the last time we interviewed you . . . '.

There is evidence to suggest that reference periods, particularly those time bounded such as 'in the last year', can be open to misinterpretation. For example, when asked about the 'last year', does that mean the last 12 months or the last calendar year? Is the current day, week or month included or excluded?

If researchers use the 'since we last interviewed you' method without also including the specific date of the last interview, respondents may be further disadvantaged as they may not recall when the last interview was, particularly if it was a long time ago.

Seam bias

Seam bias is a problem that occurs exclusively with longitudinal studies, where estimates of change across the 'seam' (the seam being the point between two waves of a longitudinal study) are far greater than estimates of change that are measured within the reference period of a single survey ('within waves'); specifically, too many changes are seen at the seam and too few within a wave. Seam bias is a form of measurement error that can impact analyses estimating change. Given that the primary goal of most longitudinal studies is to measure change across time accurately, seam bias can be a big problem.

Seam bias appears to occur independent of most design factors of studies – that is to say, it doesn't matter whether the gap between the waves of a longitudinal study or the mode in which the survey is conducted.

By way of example, seam bias has often been found to occur in surveys that capture information about employment. Employment status and transitions between different employment status and different employment circumstances, such as job roles, are key to many longitudinal studies. As such, measuring this accurately is crucial.

What is often seen is that within a reference period asked about (such as the date of the last interview), relatively low levels of changes in employment status or circumstances are reported by respondents. However, across the 'seam' of two waves of a longitudinal study, much larger rates of change are recorded. This is unlikely to reflect the true picture – it is extremely unlikely that people change their employment status or circumstances only at the point when they are interviewed in a longitudinal study. Instead, seam bias is a form of measurement error introduced by the nature of a longitudinal study combined with recall issues of respondents.

Many reasons have been put forward to explain why seam bias may occur. First, as alluded to above, respondent recall and memory issues may contribute to seam bias. Respondents are usually asked to record all changes that have taken place during the period since their last interview. As covered previously in this chapter, there are a number of recall issues that may be at play, and, particularly in relation to seam bias, it is likely that most respondents remember recent events more clearly and fail to remember accurately what happened longer ago (earlier in the reference period), which may contribute to the increased changes at the seams that are observed.

A second process that may contribute to seam bias is **satisficing**. Satisficing is essentially a strategy whereby respondents use short-cuts in order to provide a response that they think will appear to be acceptable, rather than providing an optimal response. Satisficing behaviour may be more prevalent when the task at hand is cognitively challenging or burdensome to a respondent. There are two aspects of this at play here. First, it may be cognitively challenging for a respondent to think back into the past and provide details of employment changes and transitions, so in order to provide a satisfactory response, they simply report no change across the reference period asked about (which could be seen as a satisfactory response – it is perfectly plausible that there was no change). Second, and pertinent to the longitudinal context, respondents may have learned that if they report a change, they are likely to be asked a number of follow-up questions. Using the employment example again, if they report changing their job, they may be asked for their new job title and responsibilities, information about the company they are employed by and details of the industry they work in. Rather than report change and face the additional questions, some respondents may inaccurately report stability to reduce the interview burden on themselves. This may cause inflated stability within wave and inflated instability across waves – seam bias.

The third theory that may explain seam bias, or at least contribute to it, relates to factors that are external to the respondent – namely, the interviewer and researchers doing post-interview coding. Interviewer inconsistencies across waves of a longitudinal study or post-interview processing can introduce error, which translates into the occurrence of seam bias. Going back to the now familiar example of employment, very often when respondents describe their occupation, it is not what they say that is used most commonly in analysis, but rather an occupation code that is assigned based on how they have described their job. If there are inconsistencies in the way that interviewers or coders assign these codes, seam bias may occur.

There are a multitude of studies that demonstrate the existence of seam bias in various longitudinal studies around the world. Rips and colleagues (2003) took this one stage further, investigating whether they could experimentally manipulate conditions to demonstrate seam bias and delve a little further into possible reasons for its occurrence.

Research spotlight

Rips, L.J., Conrad, F.G. and Fricker, S.S. (2003) 'Straightening the seam effect in panel surveys'

Rips and colleagues noticed the mounting evidence that seam bias existed in longitudinal studies, reflecting that previous research put this down to either underreporting of changes within the reference period asked about or overreporting of changes across the seam. In order to delve into this further, they devised a series of experiments that allowed them to look at the accuracy of respondent reports.

Their findings were striking. First, they were able to demonstrate a seam effect. More interestingly, this seam effect occurred for different types of recall - whether a question had previously appeared in the questionnaire or events had already happened - but also that the effect was present for different question grouping and orders. However, they discovered that the seam effect size is different, depending on the apparent difficulty of the recall task at hand; as the demands on memory increase, so does the size of the seam effect.

The researchers theorise that as respondents forget/fail to recall something, they tend to give the same response to each interval asked about in the reference period, even when they know that change has occurred. Ultimately, they conclude that the seam effect depends on multiple related cognitive factors.

As with the other issues of respondent recall and memory, understanding why seam bias may occur can help us to design studies in a way that minimise its occurrence and impact. The section below on study design outlines some of the design choices we could make to reduce the measure error caused by seam bias and other recall issues.

DESIGNING A STUDY TO MINIMISE RECALL PROBLEMS

Many features of longitudinal study design may impact on recall problems. Some of these may have become obvious through the discussion of types of recall issues in the previous section and others perhaps less so. This section will briefly discuss the main design factors that could influence recall issues and suggest some design choices that could be made to minimise the impact of recall issues on error in a longitudinal study.

Retrospective vs. prospective

The overarching study design is the first major design issue that could play into the likelihood and level of recall issues a study is faced with. Retrospective designs, which may ask respondents to recall events from many years ago, are likely to be more prone to bias caused by recall issues than prospective studies, whereas recall windows are likely to be much shorter.

As such, if the research questions of interest allow, it is better to start with a prospective study design to minimise measurement error caused by recall from the outset. However, often that isn't practical. As such, there are some additional design choices that could be made to minimise bias in retrospective studies, which are discussed below.

Time between interviews

One should always bear in mind the length of time between interviews when both designing a longitudinal study and also when assessing the quality of data collected by a longitudinal study. Generally, the longer period of time for which a respondent is required to recall events or behaviours, the more opportunity there is for recall bias to be introduced. This is particularly true if events are less likely to be salient to a respondent.

However, there are some design features that could be built into a study to reduce the impact of a large amount of time between the waves of a longitudinal study. The next two sections discuss two such choices that could help – namely, decisions around which reference periods to use and how to frame them, and a technique called '**dependent interviewing**', which is an opportunity unique to longitudinal studies.

Reference periods

Related to the time between interviews, care should be given to the reference periods over which respondents are required to recall events. As discussed previously, if reference periods are unclear, respondents may interpret them in different ways. This could lead to respondents either erroneously failing to report things that the researcher intended or reporting things that are outside the intended period. Both result in measurement error.

As such, reference periods should be bounded by specific dates or time frames so that respondents are clear what should be included. In the longitudinal context, where researchers often ask respondents to report what has happened since the date of their last interview, provided that date is best practice, it is highly unlikely that a respondent would remember the specific date they were last interviewed.

Dependent interviewing

One technique for reducing measurement error introduced through recall issues is dependent interviewing, a method unique to longitudinal studies. Dependent interviewing is particularly effective at reducing seam effects. This form of interviewing uses information already known about the respondent to personalise the questions they receive at later waves of a study. By providing information back to the respondent about what they have said in the past, it becomes easier for them to assess whether something has changed since that point. Let's return to our employment example. A respondent at wave one of a study tells an interviewer they are currently employed as an IT technician at a large multinational corporation. When wave two of the study comes around, the interviewer is able to ask whether the respondent is still employed as an IT technician at the large multinational corporation. It is then very easy for the respondent to know first whether they are or not, but it also makes it easier to report any changes in their employment that have happened in the interim. For example, they may have left the multinational corporation shortly after the wave one interview for an IT technician position at a local family firm and then moved on to a completely different career as an estate agent. If the interview question had not incorporated the responses the participant gave at the first interview, they may have forgotten that their first job change (same role, different company) occurred since the first interview and failed to report it.

The advent of computer-assisted interviewing has made dependent interviewing possible and it has become an increasingly common technique to increase accuracy in reporting.

Dependent interviewing is a technique that the Survey of Income and Program Participation (SIPP) introduced in 2004 in an effort to combat seam bias. SIPP is a panel study interested in various measures of employment, income, education and training in the US, asking respondents to report on the outcomes of interest at a monthly level. Moore and colleagues (2009) describe the effect the introduction of dependent interviewing had on seam bias.

Research spotlight

Moore, J., Bates, N., Pascale, J. and Okon, A. (2009) 'Tackling seam bias through questionnaire design'

The Survey of Income and Program Participation (SIPP) is a panel study in the US that provides information at a national level on income, poverty and wealth, as well as participation in various government programmes and their effects. Given the topics covered and the necessity to have accurate information about periods of employment, programme participation, such as the use of food stamps, and so on, seam bias is a concern.

In 2001, SIPP introduced dependent-like interviewing, where respondents were reminded of answers they had given previously, but the follow-up questioning reverted back to standard questions with no reference to previous answers in the question stem, nor framed in such a way that asked explicitly about continuation or change. Then in 2004, SIPP started using 'true' dependent interviewing, feeding forward what the respondent had reported at their previous interview into the current interview and asking if that had continued into the first month of the period asked about in the current interview. Follow-up questions were then asked to ascertain whether things had remained stable or changed through each month of the current interview's reference period (with some slight variations in procedure dependent on the specific question). There were two areas of questioning where the interviewing techniques remained stable between 2001 and 2004 - which is important later when we discuss the results.

The introduction of dependent interviewing was found to be a success. Seam bias reduced substantially between the 2001 estimates (with the dependent-like techniques) and the 2004 estimates captured using dependent interviewing techniques. The researchers made 45 comparisons of estimates at the seams and found in all cases reduced estimates in the 2004 data, 42 of those reductions being statistically significant.

Notably, the two areas where questions were asked in the same way in the 2001 and 2004 panels shows no differences in estimates between the two datasets. This suggests that the differences seen in estimates after the introduction of dependent interviewing in 2004 were the result of the change in procedure, rather than spurious change or linked to change in other characteristics of the questionnaire, respondent or external context.

The dependent interviewing also led to increased reports of change away from the seam. Earlier in this chapter in the introduction to seam bias, we saw that the bias doesn't just cause too many changes at the seam, but also causes too few within a survey wave. The SIPP experience demonstrates this.

However, the authors note that seam bias is still evident in SIPP. Despite the large improvements seen through the introduction of dependent interviewing, there still appears to be too many changes observed at the seam.

STUDY **PROFILE**

Survey of Income and Program Participation (SIPP)

Established: 1983.

Country: United States.

Sampling unit: household.

Sample size at base: 19,878 households.

Frequency of interviews: rotating panel, with households taking part three times a year. Duration in the panel varies depending on recruitment year.

Participants: US residents aged 15 and over.

(Continued)

Topics covered: income, programme participation, economic well-being, family dynamics, education, assets, health insurance, childcare and food security.

Methods of data collection: face-to-face; telephone.

Data availability: data are available on the UC Census Bureau website.

More information: www.census.gov/programs-surveys/sipp.html

HOW TO ASSESS RECALL BIAS

Now that we have explored types of recall bias, theories for what may cause this type of error and best practice techniques in study and survey design to minimise the occurrence of these issues, the next step is understanding how we might assess recall bias. Unfortunately, there isn't an easy solution here.

Short of using a secondary data source, taken as gold standard to assess survey responses against, there isn't much to be done to correct bias caused by recall issues once it has already occurred. Instead, as described above, if you are designing a longitudinal study, it is important to bear in mind the aspects of design that may increase recall bias and try to minimise them in the design itself. As a user of longitudinal research, it is important to assess how likely you think it is to have occurred and whether it could potentially be causing big changes in estimates (look at recall length, question type, interviewing techniques, etc.). If you have suspicions that bias caused by recall issues may be at play, be up front about it when writing about longitudinal data.

CONCLUSIONS

As longitudinal studies tend to be primarily interested in change over time, and how past events and experiences shape future outcomes, it is common for respondents to be asked to recall events since their previous interview. However, as we have seen, there are a number of issues with recall and respondent memory. Respondents may fail to recall certain events; less commonly, they may recall things that never actually happened or they may recall events imprecisely, particularly the timings of those events.

In the longitudinal context, there exists the unique phenomenon of seam bias, where the design of a longitudinal study and the requirement on respondents to recall events that had happened since the last survey cause too many changes to be seen at the seam (between waves) and too few within a wave.

Recall issues can lead to measurement error in a survey. However, as these issues become more and more researched, ways to design longitudinal studies to reduce the likelihood of their occurrence have been discovered. These include considerations of retrospective versus prospective designs, reference periods and the dependent interviewing technique.

Despite these advances, error caused by faulty recall can still exist within longitudinal data, with no clear solution (beyond using a gold-standard data source against which to assess measurement error). Researchers should be mindful of these issues when using longitudinal data and transparent in their assessment of such issues.

Key learning points

- As longitudinal studies tend to be interested in change over time and past events and experiences, respondents are often asked to recall events since their previous interview. However, the human memory is not perfect and inaccurate recall can cause biases in the data collected.
- There are a number of known recall phenomenon.
    - Telescoping, where respondents perceive recent events as happening longer ago than they actually did (backward telescoping) and events from a long time ago happening more recently than they did (forward telescoping).
    - Omissions, where an event is not reported at all, either because it has been forgotten by the respondent or the respondent explicitly chooses not to report it.
    - Commissions, where events that never happened are recalled and reported.
    - Reference period misinterpretation, where the period over which a respondent is asked to recall events is not understood by all respondents in the same way or by respondents in the way the researcher intended, causing events either to be reported where they shouldn't have been or not reported where they should have been.
    - Seam bias, unique to longitudinal studies, where estimates of change across the 'seam' (between two waves of a longitudinal study) are much greater than estimates of change that are measured within the reference period of a single survey ('within waves'); too many changes are seen at the seam and too few within a wave.
- Understanding more about the contexts in which recall issues may occur and the reasons for their occurrence has led to some suggestions about how longitudinal studies might be designed to minimise incidence and impact of recall issues.
    - Retrospective versus prospective designs: retrospective designs, which may ask respondents to recall events from many years ago, are likely to be more prone to bias caused by recall issues than prospective studies, where recall windows are likely to be much shorter. As such, it is better to start with a prospective study design to minimise measurement error caused by recall from the outset (noting that this may not be possible).
    - Time between interviews: generally, the longer the period of time for which a respondent is required to recall events or behaviours, the more opportunity there is for recall bias to be introduced.
    - Reference periods: care should be taken to ensure clarity for respondents in the reference periods over which they are required to recall events. Ideally, reference periods should be bounded by specific dates or time frames.

(Continued)

- Dependent interviewing: longitudinal studies allow for information already known about the respondent to be used to personalise the questions they receive at later waves of a study. By providing information back to the respondent about what they have said in the past, it becomes easier for them to assess whether something has changed since that point.

- Assessing recall bias in a study or a dataset is a tricky issue. Short of using a secondary data source, taken as gold standard, to assess survey responses against, there isn't much to be done to correct bias caused by recall issues once it has already occurred. Instead, it is important to bear in mind the aspects of design that may increase recall bias and try to minimise them in the design itself. As a user of longitudinal research, it is important to assess how likely you think it is that recall bias occurred and whether it could potentially be causing big changes in estimates. If you have suspicions that bias caused by recall issues may be at play, be up front about it when writing about longitudinal data.

Check your understanding

1. What is recall bias and why is it a problem for longitudinal studies?
2. Briefly describe the types of recall problems that may affect a longitudinal study.
3. What are some of the reasons that seam bias may occur in a longitudinal study?
4. What are some of the study design features that could reduce recall bias in a longitudinal study?
5. When using a longitudinal dataset, what are the study design factors you would look at to assess whether recall bias could be a problem?

WANT TO FIND OUT MORE?

The resources below are great sources of additional information on the content covered in this section.

For a discussion of recall bias and strategies to minimise its impact:

Hassan, E. (2005) 'Recall bias can be a threat to retrospective and prospective research designs', *The Internet Journal of Epidemiology*, 3 (2).

For a summary of the literature on seam bias:

Callegaro, M. (2008) 'Seam effects in longitudinal surveys', *Journal of Official Statistics*, 24 (3): 387–409.

For a conceptual framework on dependent interviewing:

Jäckle, A. (2009) 'Dependent interviewing: A framework and application to current research', in Lynn, P. (ed.) *Methodology of Longitudinal Surveys*. Chichester: John Wiley & Sons.

NOTE

1. The term 'developing country' was used by the authors of the study in the title of the published article. 'Underdeveloped country' is the preferred term.

7

QUESTION TYPES, FEATURES AND COMPARABILITY

OVERVIEW OF CONTENT

This chapter will provide you with an overview of different types of close-ended question formats (where respondents are given a predetermined list of responses from which to choose), question features and a discussion on the comparability of questions that vary their features and formats. This is particularly important in a longitudinal context, when looking at the same question across multiple waves of a study in order to understand the potential impact of question design features on response.

The chapter will also introduce the issues surrounding question ordering and how decisions over the order of questions can impact on resultant data.

The chapter concludes with a section about data harmonisation – a way of looking at data from different waves within studies and across studies, and transforming it so that it is comparable.

Learning outcomes

After you have read this chapter, you will be able to:

- describe the most common types of question format, including rating scales, sliders and grids;
- describe the most common features of questions that can be varied, including scale length, direction and labelling;
- understand how the order of questions can impact response;
- understand the impact of varying question format, features and order on the longitudinal data;
- understand what is data harmonisation in a longitudinal context.

WHY ARE QUESTION FORMATS AND FEATURES IMPORTANT?

Longitudinal studies across the world employ a huge range of question types and formats; there are multiple ways of asking about the same **construct**. When using longitudinal data, a researcher should be mindful of exactly how the question they are interested in has been asked, whether it has been kept consistent across waves and the impact that might have on response and subsequent comparability with other data sources (for related information, see Chapters 8 and 9 on mode of data collection).

WHAT ARE THE MOST COMMON QUESTION FORMATS?

Questions can be formatted in a multitude of different ways. While you may think that the choice of a specific format might not make too much difference to the way that respondents answer the question, research shows that decisions around question formatting can have significant impacts on responses. In a cross-sectional context, this may not be a major concern (although, of course, there are reasons why this could be concerning, particularly if talking about comparability across different surveys). In a longitudinal context, however, the choice of question format may have larger implications. This is true when thinking about comparability within a study over time – changing the question format from one wave to the next, even if you believe the question itself hasn't changed, can impact on the data gathered and therefore conclusions drawn. It's also a concern when different formats of a question are used within a mixed-mode context in a single wave of a study (see Chapters 8, 9 and 10 on mode and mixed-mode issues for data collection).

Question formats are crucial to think about when designing or using data from both self-administered survey modes – for example, online surveys or paper questionnaires – or from interviewer-administered modes – for example, face-to-face or telephone interviews. This is because the issues of format can have an impact not just on how the respondent visually sees a question, such as in self-administered modes, but also on how an interviewer verbally presents a question to a respondent.

This section will talk through some of the most common formats for survey questions in turn, discussing how each format can impact response. The reader should be mindful of the implicit implications for longitudinal studies, where changing formats across waves may change the data collected.

Rating scales

A rating scale asks the respondent a question and gives them a defined set of response options from which they can pick to respond to the question. The response options can be laid out vertically or horizontally (depending on the mode of administration).

Let's work through an example (one that we will use for each of the different question formats, so it is easy to see the differences). Imagine you want to understand how much people trust others in their community. A reasonably common way of asking this question is as follows: 'On a scale of 1 to 5 (1 = cannot be trusted at all; 5 = can be trusted a lot), how much do you trust people in your neighbourhood?' Laid out in a typical rating scale fashion, the question would be presented as follows.

On a scale of 1 to 5 (1 = cannot be trusted at all; 5 = can be trusted a lot), how much do you trust people in your neighbourhood?

1. Cannot be trusted at all
2.
3.
4.
5. Can be trusted a lot

The respondent is then required to select one of the options 1 to 5.

Sliders

A slider is a different way of visually presenting a scale. Instead of having a question followed by a list of response options from which the respondent must pick, a slider provides the question followed by a (usually horizontal) line (the line marked with the possible response options) with a movable indicator that the respondent must slide to sit on the response they want to select.

Using the same trust example, the question in slider form is shown in Figure 7.1

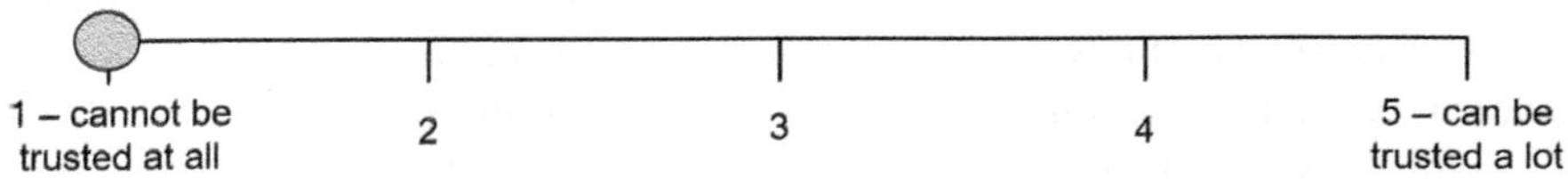

Figure 7.1 An example of a question formatted as a slider

Grids

Grids are a special form of rating scale, where many questions with the same response scale are grouped together. This may not sound like a problem – after all, they may be quicker for respondents to use to answer groups of similar questions – but there can be unintended consequences.

If a survey had a set of questions that all concerned trust and all used the same 1–5 response scale, the questions could be presented as a grid. It would look something like that shown in Figure 7.2.

	1 – cannot be trusted at all	2	3	4	5 – can be trusted a lot
... people in your neighbourhood					
... people in your family					
... people you work with					
.... strangers					

Figure 7.2 An example of a set of questions formatted as a grid

On a scale of 1 to 5 (1 = cannot be trusted at all; 5 = can be trusted a lot), how much do you trust the following people?

Respondents are required to select one option per row. This may be quicker for respondents to answer than four separate questions, but there could be unintended negative consequences too.

The main consequence is likely to be **non-differentiation** – that is, failing to read and respond to each specific question, and rather providing the same answer for every question rather than the true or accurate answer. This obviously can have a negative impact on data quality.

WHAT ARE THE MOST COMMON QUESTION FEATURES THAT CAN BE VARIED?

There are many common features of a question that can be varied. This can include the scale length, the scale direction or labelling on a scale, and each of these things can apply to all the question formats described in the previous section Let's think through each of these features in turn.

Scale length

Scale length refers to the number of response options from which respondents can choose when answering a scale question. Scales, theoretically, can be of any length (although having, for example, a scale from which respondents can choose one of 47 points is probably not the wisest decision). Let's use an example of community cohesion.

The following example has five options from which a respondent can choose.

Thinking about your local area, to what extent do you agree or disagree that people from different backgrounds get along well together?

- Strongly agree
- Agree
- Neither agree nor disagree
- Disagree
- Strongly disagree

However, we could choose to have a smaller number of scale points, such as three:

- Agree
- Neither agree nor disagree
- Disagree

Or a larger number, such as seven:

- Strongly agree
- Moderately agree
- Slightly agree
- Neither agree nor disagree
- Slightly disagree
- Moderately disagree
- Strongly disagree

This could have implications for how respondents answer the question. However, the impact of these implications in part can depend on how the data are analysed. For example, if you're just interested in comparing people who agree with the statement with people who disagree, in the five- and seven-point scales, you would code all those who had any level of agreement as 'agree' and all those who disagreed to any extent as 'disagree'. This would likely remove or at least reduce issues with the length of the scale. On the other hand, if you're interested in the nuance and want to keep the original responses in the analysis, it could have differing effects depending on how long the scale is.

A specific extension of this idea concerns the midpoint of a scale. In all the examples covered in this section so far, regardless of scale length, the response options contained a midpoint. This is the neutral option – 'neither agree nor disagree' – in the examples used. However, the scale doesn't have to contain a midpoint at all. Rather than allow a respondent to indicate that they are neutral on an issue, a scale could force the respondent to make a substantive choice. By way of example, the previous question can be set up in this way.

Thinking about your local area, to what extent do you agree or disagree that people from different backgrounds get along well together?

- Strongly agree
- Agree
- Disagree
- Strongly disagree

Respondents must choose a response that indicates that they either agree or disagree with the statement.

A midpoint can be helpful. For issues that respondents may reasonably not have an opinion either way, the midpoint can give them an appropriate response to use to answer the question. For example, if you asked people what they thought about a proposed new policy related to welfare, they may genuinely not have an opinion. The midpoint allows them to express that.

On the other hand, a midpoint may work against you. It can be seen as an 'easy' answer for respondents to give. Even if they do have an opinion about a particular topic, choosing the midpoint is an easy way out without having to really think about where they would place themselves on the response scale available to them. Alternatively, it may also be seen as a more socially acceptable answer than their true feelings. If social desirability bias is at play (see Chapter 5 for more information on social desirability bias), a respondent may not want to choose a substantive answer on one end of the scale or the other, because they perceive their answer would not be socially desirable. Instead, they could use the midpoint to provide an answer which they think would be seen as more acceptable, even though it doesn't represent their true views.

By including or removing a midpoint from a scale, researchers risk changing the distribution of responses to a question. In a longitudinal context, this is particularly problematic if the question format changes from one wave to the next. Any changes in the distribution of responses that are given may be down to the change in question format rather than a true change in the population.

Using an experimental approach, Johns (2005) examines this issue, looking specifically at the inclusion or exclusion of a scale mid-point on the subsequent data collected.

Research spotlight

Johns, R. (2005) 'One size doesn't fit all: Selecting response scales for attitude items'

Robert Johns was interested in the implications of including or not including a midpoint in the context of a five-point agree-disagree scale in order to maximise the validity of data collected using these scales. He used data from an experiment included in the British Social Attitudes study, looking at agree-disagree scales with and without a midpoint on topics pertaining to economic attitudes. Some respondents saw the scales with a midpoint included and some saw the same questions with the scales modified slightly to remove the midpoint.

After doing various comparisons (which also included a split-ballot experiment including and omitting an explicit 'don't know response'), he found first that where a midpoint in a scale is offered, a relatively large proportion of respondents chose it. Comparing responses to when a midpoint is offered to when it is not, removing the midpoint can cause shifts in reported attitudes overall - that is to say, people are forced into substantive categories, which changes the overall picture shown in the data (thereby changing what researchers would conclude when looking at the data).

Ultimately, he offers two recommendations for survey designers. First, where a survey question asks about a topic which many respondents are likely not to have an opinion on or be indifferent to, then a midpoint is useful and should be included. By not including a midpoint, people are forced to respond in a way that suggests they have an opinion, where in reality they might not. This can skew the data. Second, where a question is prone to socially desirable responding, then removing the midpoint is helpful. By including a midpoint, true attitudes are missed, as people who have views which they perceive as being socially undesirable are likely to choose the midpoint, masking true attitudes.

Scale direction

The next feature of a scale which could be varied is the direction -that is to say, the scale could be presented with the positive response first or it could be the negative response. The same applies to response scales that try to quantify something, so the high value could be first or the low value could be first.

Using the community cohesion example and the five-point scale for simplicity, respondents could be presented with the question with the positive response first.

Thinking about your local area, to what extent do you agree or disagree that people from different backgrounds get along well together?

- Strongly agree
- Agree
- Neither agree nor disagree
- Disagree
- Strongly disagree

Respondents could alternatively be presented with the negative response first.

Thinking about your local area, to what extent do you agree or disagree that people from different backgrounds get along well together?

- Strongly disagree
- Disagree
- Neither disagree nor agree
- Agree
- Strongly agree

You might think that this has no impact on the way that respondents answer questions. However, that's not necessarily the case. The **primacy effect** – the theory that respondents may choose the first response they come across which reflects their views when they are presented with a response scale visually – is often cited as one of the primary reasons that scale direction could cause differences in responses. If respondents are reading response options from top to bottom in a vertically ordered scale, as our examples above are laid out, and they agree with the statement, if the positive responses are first and they see 'strongly agree' first, they may pick that. However, if the options start with the disagree statement, the response they see first when reading down the list which reflects their views is 'agree', so they may be inclined to choose that. Instantly, we see there would be two different responses from one person depending on how the scale is ordered.

In a longitudinal context, there is a particular implication of this. If in one wave of a study a question is presented with the positive response option first, but in another wave of the same study the negative response option is first, there could be an impact on the data – that is to say, it may appear that responses (and by implication, attitudes or behaviours) change over time, when in fact it could be to do with the change in question design and not a true change. Readers are advised to look carefully at the question format and design when analysing longitudinal data, so that any changes in the ways that questions are asked are spotted.

However, it may be that scale direct effects don't hold true for all forms of response scale and for all questions. In order to investigate the circumstances under which scale direction has an impact on resultant data, Yan and colleagues (2018) looked at secondary data sources to try to establish conditions under which scale direction has an impact on data.

Research spotlight

Yan, T., Keusch, F. and He, L. (2018) 'The impact of question and scale characteristics on scale direction effects'

Using data from the American National Election Studies (ANES), Yan and colleagues set out to investigate what drove differences in responses to rating scales that were ordered either positively or negatively. They were interested specifically in where there are features of the questions that were associated with scale direction effects, features of the scale and whether mode played a part in this phenomenon. The ANES had included experiments in some of their surveys that randomly varied scale direction, allowing the researchers to robustly look at the resultant effect of scale direction.

Yan and colleagues found first a primacy effect overall in the data - respondents were more likely to choose a response in the first half of the scale they saw than the second half, regardless of whether the positive or negative responses were presented first (not a surprising result, given that some previous literature had demonstrated this). However, this was not true for all scales examined.

They then turned to looking at the question and scale features. They discovered that non-attitudinal items were more prone to scale direction effects than attitudinal items. Scale direction effects were also more common when the question under investigation was included in the first half of the survey compared with those in the second half of the survey. Scale direction was also associated with scale length. Scales with more response options were more prone to direction effects than those with fewer options.

Looking at mode, the authors discovered that scale direction effects were more common in survey items in self-administered modes (in this case, on the web and in audio-Computer-Assisted Self-Interviewing, or audio-CASI) than those interviewed via an interviewer using Computer-Assisted Personal Interviewing (CAPI).

Ultimately, the authors recommended that in order for researchers to be able to assess the impact of scale direction, scale order and placement of questions should be rotated when researchers are designing questionnaires. This would allow users of the data to control for the effects of scale direction.

Scale labelling

There are two types of labels that could be varied on a response scale. First, when using a response scale, it is possible to label some or all of the response options. Sometimes, just the two extremes of a scale are labelled (known as end-labelling) or every point on the scale could be labelled. The second variation is which type of labels are used. These could be numerical, written descriptors or some combination of both.

Turning once again to the community cohesion example, a fully labelled version of this question is one we have already seen.

Thinking about your local area, to what extent do you agree or disagree that people from different backgrounds get along well together?

- Strongly agree
- Agree
- Neither agree nor disagree
- Disagree
- Strongly disagree

However, this could also be formatted using end-labels only.

Thinking about your local area, to what extent do you agree or disagree that people from different backgrounds get along well together?

1. Strongly agree
2.
3.
4.
5. Strongly disagree

While these questions may appear to be essentially the same and you might think that asking respondents either version would yield the same results, that's not necessarily true. Let's look at why that might be. What do the numbers 2, 3 and 4 mean to respondents? By fully labelling all the scale points, all respondents are using the same reference to answer the question. By using only numerical labels, each scale point is open to interpretation. The particularly problematic response option could be the middle one – option 3 in the above example. In the fully labelled version, we gave this the label 'neither agree nor disagree' – something of a neutral response. However, without this label, respondents could interpret what we mean in various ways. It could be seen as an option that indicates they have mixed views – in some ways they agree with the statement, but in others they disagree. Or respondents might use this as a 'don't know' option, where they feel they don't have enough of an opinion about an issue to make an informed choice of response.

In general, it is considered best practice to verbally label all points on a response scale. However, this does depend on the precise scale being used. On an agree–disagree scale or similar, it is advisable to label all points. It is less useful on a longer scale – for example, when asking respondents to rate something on a 1–10 scale.

Maitland (2009) provides a nice overview of the issues around scale labelling in the context of attitudinal questions, discussing both theory and practice.

Research spotlight

Maitland, A. (2009) 'Should I label all scale points or just the end points for attitudinal questions?'

Maitland aimed to answer the question which titled his article around scale labelling - should all scale points be labelled when asking an attitudinal question or just the end points?

He argued that the most important consideration around labelling was whether labelling response scales adds clarity. Ultimately, the labels should provide clarity for respondents, whether they are used for all scale points or just the end points. For many respondents, words may provide more clarity than numbers alone.

However, the length of the scale also plays a part in the decision to label scale points. Labelling all points of a five-point scale is easily achievable; labelling all points on an 11-point scale may be less so. It is very difficult to come up with 11 distinct verbal labels for an attitudinal scale.

Reviewing the existing literature on scale labelling, Maitland notes that many studies have found that fully labelled scales produce data of higher quality than partially labelled scales. He points to two reasons why this may be the case. First, labelling can increase reliability and validity of data, which may be driven particularly by those with lower levels of education. Verbal labelling can increase the understanding of the task and therefore improve data quality. Second, fully labelling a scale can reduce the negative effects of other question features, again improving data quality.

Additionally, the literature provides guidance on how labels should be selected. Some evidence suggests that symmetrical labels work best, increasing both reliability and validity. Verbal labels that match the numerical labels on a scale are also preferred. If the end point of a scale are the only ones labelled, the choice of label is important; they should be fixed or absolute points - for example, 'completely' or 'fully'.

Ultimately, Maitland argues that labelling should be chosen to ensure that it makes the task for the respondent most clearly defined, regardless of the choice of specific labels or a labelling strategy. In general, fully labelled scales are preferable to end-labels alone, but this decision is dependent on scale length, interview mode and the population of interest.

WHY IS QUESTION ORDER IMPORTANT?

The order in which questions are presented to respondents can have an impact on the responses that respondents give to those questions. In the longitudinal context, this can mean that changing the ordering of questions between waves could show either change or stability where in reality it doesn't exist.

One of the most common theories as to why changing question order can impact on responses is called **priming**. Put simply, this means that exposure to a particular topic can have a subsequent impact on someone's thoughts about the next thing they are exposed to. To give an example, a respondent may be asked a set of questions about their experiences of being a victim of crime, followed by a question about how safe they feel in their neighbourhood. By thinking explicitly about their experiences of victimisation, they may reflect on the general question about safety afterwards and not feel particularly safe in their neighbourhood. However, if these questions were asked the other way round, with the general safety question first and the victimisation questions second, the responses to the safety question may be different (as the respondent may not have been thinking about their personal experiences of crime). To take the example further, if in one wave of a longitudinal study the general safety question is asked first and in the next wave the safety question is asked second, different responses may be given. This could lead a researcher to concluding that people feel less safe in the current wave than they did in the previous wave. In reality, the fact that the ordering of questions has changed may have driven this change in responses, creating a false decrease in apparent feelings of safety.

The issue of question order was investigated by researchers interested in responses to a question on self-rated health in the English Longitudinal Study of Ageing (ELSA). Self-rated health was a key measure in the ELSA study, so it was important to understand how respondents might answer it differently depending on where in the questionnaire the question was asked. Bowling and Windsor (2008) summarised their findings in a journal article on the topic.

Research spotlight

Bowling, A. and Windsor, J. (2008) 'The effects of question order and response-choice on self-rated health status in the English Longitudinal Study of Ageing (ELSA)'

As Bowling and Windsor note in their article, self-rated health is one of the most common ways of measuring health status worldwide. As such, it is important that the responses to the question are accurate and reliable. The English Longitudinal Study of Ageing (ELSA) is a longitudinal study looking at the population of England aged 50 and over for the perspective of health, well-being and ageing. A self-reported health measure is crucial for a study such as this.

However, research shows that where a question is placed in a questionnaire can have an impact on the responses gained to the question. A split-ballot experiment embedded into the first wave of ELSA enabled examination of this issue. Two self-rated health questions were shown to each respondent. One asked respondents to rate their health on a scale of 'excellent' to 'poor' and the other used a scale of 'very good' to 'very bad'. A random half of respondents saw the 'excellent' to 'poor' question before a wider module of health questions (and the 'very good' to 'very bad' scale after), and the other half saw the questions in the other order. This allows a comparison of both question order effects and scale wording effect.

The authors found that when the 'very good' to 'very bad' question was placed after the more detailed health module, respondents were likely to be more positive about their health. The same was true with the 'excellent' to 'poor' scale. They found this to be true of all age groups surveyed, except those aged 80 and over. This was also particularly true of those who appeared to be in good health (as assessed by the more objective health questions included in the survey module). This suggests that answering a block of objective health questions influences responses to a self-rated health measure, although it should be noted that in this instance, effect sizes were reasonably small.

Bowling and Windsor go on to suggest that a self-rated health question in particular should be asked before a more objective set of questions on health in order to avoid the latter having an impact on the former.

STUDY **PROFILE**

English Longitudinal Study of Ageing (ELSA)

Established: 2002.

Country: England.

Sampling unit: individuals.

Sample size at base: 12,100 individuals.

Frequency of interviews: every two years.

Participants: individuals aged 50 and over living in England.

Topics covered: health, economic and social circumstances.

Methods of data collection: face-to-face, self-completion, telephone and online.

Data availability: data are available via the UK Data Archive.

More information: www.elsa-project.ac.uk/

WHAT DOES THIS ALL MEAN FOR LONGITUDINAL STUDIES?

This chapter has shown so far that there are many different ways of formatting survey questions, all of which can have implications for how respondents answer them. You might be thinking 'so what?' In a longitudinal context, the answer to 'so what?' is that choices of question formats within studies across waves and across different studies, as alluded to at various points previously, can have consequences for the data. These consequences may not be trivial.

Within a study, it might be that the study aims to capture consistent information at different points in time across the same attitudes, opinions or behaviours. Indeed, that's often the point of a longitudinal study. However, if the format of a question is varied across different waves, this can impact how respondents answer questions. It may be that it appears that there has been change on particular measures across time, when in fact this change is driven by changing the question format as opposed to being driven by true change. You might think, 'Well, that's not going to happen, surely study designers make sure they use the exact same question and format in each wave of the study'. True – it's very often the case that longitudinal study designers do keep the same format each time. But, more recently, many studies have either transitioned to a mixed-mode design or used different modes at different waves of data collection (see Chapters 8, 9 and 10 for discussions of mode and mixed-mode approaches). Often, different modes necessitate slightly different versions or variations of questions being used.

Study designers, in a longitudinal context, can choose either to keep the exact same version of a question across modes or they may choose to optimise the question design to fit with the mode of choice. Either choice should be noted by researchers using longitudinal data. Implementing the exact same question may cause issues where it is not designed for a particular mode, and optimising the question design to fit a particular mode may cause comparability issues. Researchers should look carefully at question design choices when using longitudinal data to be aware of the impact this could have on their analysis and conclusions.

Harmonisation

You may have read the chapter up to this point and wondered, 'Well, what can we do about all of this?' Fortunately, help is at hand. The research community have become increasingly aware of comparability issues within different waves of longitudinal studies and across different studies. As a result, more and more effort and resource are being spent on harmonisation.

Harmonisation, in its simplest form, is a way of looking at data from different waves within studies and across studies, and transforming it in some way so that it is comparable. While space will not be dedicated here to outlining exactly how that is done (in part because it depends very heavily on the topic under investigation and the specific questions of interest), it is valuable for the reader to know where to look for harmonisation information.

A good example is the CLOSER resource in the UK. CLOSER is bringing together longitudinal studies from across the UK in order to maximise the use, value and impact of the data from those studies. One of their key workstreams is in harmonisation. They are working on different topic areas across all the studies to produce datasets that are harmonised, meaning different ways of asking questions about the same topics can be used in conjunction with one another, overcoming issues of comparability.

Also, a great deal of other work has been conducted in order to harmonise longitudinal data on a smaller scale. It is worth researchers establishing whether data they are planning to use from a longitudinal study or across different studies has already been harmonised prior to embarking on analysis.

STUDY **PROFILE**

CLOSER

Country: United Kingdom.

Participating studies:

- 1958 National Child Development Study (NCDS).
- 1970 British Cohort Study (BCS70).
- Avon Longitudinal Study of Parents and Children (ALSPAC, also known as 'Children of the 90s').
- Born in Bradford.
- English Longitudinal Study of Ageing (ELSA).
- Generation Scotland (also known as the Scottish Family Health Study).
- Growing up in Scotland (GUS).
- Health and Employment After Fifty (HEAF).
- Hertfordshire Cohort Study.
- Longitudinal Survey of Young People in England: Cohort 2 (also known as Our Future).
- Millennium Cohort Study (also known as Child of the New Century).
- Next Steps (previously known as the Longitudinal Study of Young People in England).
- Northern Ireland Cohort for the Longitudinal Study of Ageing (NICOLA).
- ONS Longitudinal Study.
- Southampton Women's Survey.
- Whitehall II.
- Wirral Child Health and Development Study (also known as the First Steps Study).

Data availability: harmonised data from participating studies are available via the UK Data Archive.

More information: www.closer.ac.uk/

Key learning points

- Longitudinal studies across the world employ a huge range of question types and formats; there are multiple ways of asking about the same construct.
- When using longitudinal data, a researcher should be mindful of exactly how the question they are interested in has been asked, whether it has been kept consistent across waves, and the impact that might have on response and subsequent comparability with other data sources.
- Questions can be formatted in multiple different ways. The key ones are:
  - scales;
  - sliders;
  - grids.
- There are many common features of a question which can be varied. The key ones are:
  - scale length;
  - scale direction;
  - scale labelling.
- Varying question formats and features across waves of a longitudinal study can have unintended impacts on the data. Variation in questions between waves could show either change or stability where in reality it doesn't exist.
- The order in which questions are presented to respondents can have an impact on the responses that respondents give to those questions.
- Harmonisation can help to overcome some of the problems with different question features and designs, by transforming data to ensure that it is comparable.

Check your understanding

1. What are the advantages and disadvantages of arranging survey questions in a grid format?
2. When would including a midpoint in a scale be useful?
3. Imagine you are designing a question to measure trust in the police. How would you format the question? Think about the format, as well as the response scale features.
4. Describe priming as a theory for the manifestation of question order effects.
5. Why is harmonisation helpful for longitudinal data?

WANT TO FIND OUT MORE?

The resources below are great sources of additional information on the content covered in this section.

For evidence on the effects of different types of scale design:

Converse, J.M. and Presser, S. (1986) *Survey Questions: Handcrafting the Standardized Questionnaire*. Thousand Oaks, CA: Sage Publications.

For more information on how to write effective survey questions:

Fowler, F.J. and Cosenza, C. (2008) 'Writing effective questions', in de Leeuw, E., Hox, J.J. and Dillman, D.A. (eds) *International Handbook of Survey Methodology*. New York: Psychology Press.

8

MODE OF DATA COLLECTION: VERBAL MODES

OVERVIEW OF CONTENT

This chapter will provide you with an overview of the main verbal modes of data collection – namely, face-to-face interviewing and telephone surveys. It will explain the advantages and disadvantages of each method.

Some of the advantages and disadvantages pertinent to longitudinal studies that are introduced in this chapter will be expanded on further in separate chapters in this book, and this is signposted where necessary. Chapter 10, on the implications of design choices for longitudinal studies, will also explore some of these issues further.

Learning outcomes

After you have read this chapter, you will be able to:

- understand why different data-collection modes are used in longitudinal research;
- explain the benefits of using computerised rather than paper-based data collection;
- describe the benefits of carrying out research using verbal data-collection modes;
- describe the drawbacks of verbal modes.

VERBAL DATA-COLLECTION MODES

Over time, the number of methods by which longitudinal studies can collect data from their participants has increased. Historically, the vast majority of studies conducted face-to-face interviews, where interviewers would visit people in their homes and ask them questions.

As more people started to own telephones, some studies chose to collect data in this way instead, partly in a bid to reduce costs. Rather than having interviewers travel over vast geographic areas, they became centralised, working from an interviewing call centre.

As technology has developed and laptop computers became more commonplace, studies transitioned to using computer-assisted interviews, so rather than interviewers writing information onto paper, responses were entered directly into a computer. This is true of both face-to-face interviews and telephone interviews.

In addition, surveys have been conducted by paper, usually mailed to respondents who are then asked to post them back. With the rise of the internet, many surveys have now transitioned online, collecting data using web questionnaires.

The method by which survey data is collected is known as the 'mode'. Due to the wide variety of modes now utilised by longitudinal studies, researchers should be aware of the method used to capture data and the impact this may have on responses. Of particular importance in a longitudinal context is whether the mode has changed over time or a mixed-mode approach has been used, where different respondents may be interviewed in different modes within the same wave of a study.

The following two chapters focus on the four major modes, grouped together into verbal modes (this chapter) and visual modes (Chapter 9).

Face-to-face interviews

Face-to-face interviews have traditionally been the 'mode of choice' for surveys, both longitudinal and cross-sectional. Many major longitudinal studies have sent interviewers to respondents' homes to collect data using a face-to-face interview. Historically, responses were captured on paper, but as technology developed, the use of computers became commonplace. Interviews conducted by interviewers using computers are known as 'computer-assisted personal interviews', or CAPI.

CAPI has many benefits over paper questionnaires:

1. It allows for complex **questionnaire routing**. This means that questions can be tailored based on responses to previous questions. For example, if a respondent says they voted in the last national election in their country, the next question could ask which party or candidate they voted for. If they said they didn't vote, the question about which party or candidate would be skipped. While this is possible on paper, it is easier for interviewers using CAPI as they don't have to work out the correct routing themselves. The example given is a simple one – this can become far more complex when collecting information about things such as employment or income.

2. Data quality checks can be implemented. The questionnaire can be programmed to spot inconsistent or unlikely responses and flag to the interviewer the potential problem. As an example, if a respondent is 21 years old, but reports having a child aged 15, the program could flag that this is an unlikely combination and ask the interviewer to check the details with the respondent. An interviewer conducting a face-to-face interview, but using paper to record the answers may miss these inconsistencies.
3. Historical information can be 'fed forward'. In the context of a longitudinal survey, responses respondents have given in previous interviews can be automatically fed into a future survey. The benefits of this are twofold. First, respondents can be shown the information already held and asked if it is still correct, rather than them having to provide the same information again (see Chapter 6 for a discussion of this in relation to recall and seam bias). Second, if the respondent has already provided certain information in the past, the questionnaire can be programmed to skip questions that they don't need to answer again.
4. Data processing is easier. Rather than having to manually enter the paper questionnaire responses into a computer-based or punch-card system, the data are already in an electronic format, ready for processing and use. Removing the manual entry stage also reduces the risk of errors being made in input.

Benefits of using face-to-face interviews

There are benefits of using face-to-face interviews over other methods of data collection, such as telephone or web questionnaires.

Increased response rates

One of the biggest concerns when conducting a survey is the response rate. Researchers want to aim for as high a response rate as possible in a bid to reduce bias caused by particular groups of people not participating (although it should be noted that bias is not necessarily reduced when response rates are increased). There is a lot of evidence to suggest that face-to-face interviews achieve higher response rates than other modes of data collection. Hox and de Leeuw (1994) explore this issue in more detail.

Research spotlight

Hox, J.J. and de Leeuw, E.D. (1994) 'A comparison of nonresponse in mail, telephone, and face-to-face surveys'

Hox and de Leeuw conducted a meta-analysis to assess response rates across different modes of survey data collection. A meta-analysis involves looking at many different studies that examine the same topic to gauge trends. In this case, the authors reviewed

(Continued)

45 different studies that had explicitly compared the response rates between face-to-face, mail or telephone surveys.

They found that the face-to-face surveys they included in the analysis had the highest response rates at 70.3 per cent. Telephone surveys had the next highest with 67.2 per cent and mail the lowest at 61.3 per cent. While there are some interaction effects - namely, the year the survey was conducted and the type of sample surveyed – face-to-face still came out on top.

This shows that if a high response rate is the aim, face-to-face interviews may be an easier way of achieving it than using telephone or mail surveys.

Interviewer rapport

Having a real interviewer present can encourage completion of a survey. Interviewers can build rapport with the respondent, encouraging them to answer all the questions and reassuring them if they have any concerns around the questionnaire content or confidentiality and privacy. As well as increasing the response rate overall, it can also increase the response to individual survey questions. See Chapter 5 for information on how interviewer rapport is particularly important in a longitudinal context.

Interviewer support

If the respondent struggles to answer a question, the interviewer is able to provide help. For example, a respondent may be unclear about the meaning of a question or a particular term used. In a face-to-face survey, an interviewer is on hand to provide clarification about what the question is asking. This may improve data quality.

Disadvantages of using face-to-face interviews

As well as the advantages, there are some disadvantages to using face-to-face interviews over other modes of data collection, depending on the context.

Social desirability bias

Social desirability bias is the tendency of some respondents to respond to a question in a way that they feel is socially acceptable or desirable, even when the response isn't accurate. This can lead to underreporting of attitudes or behaviours that are seen as negative or undesirable, and overreporting of desirable behaviours and attitudes. Heerwegh (2009) explores this issue by comparing face-to-face and web survey responses using an experimental design.

Research spotlight

Heerwegh, D. (2009) 'Mode differences between face-to-face and web surveys: An experimental investigation of data quality and social desirability effects'

Heerwegh set out to investigate the differences in responses to face-to-face and web surveys using an experimental design. He collected data from a set of respondents who were first all interviewed face-to-face. Then a randomly selected proportion completed the final part of the survey using the web and the remaining respondents completed the final section of the interview face-to-face. The final set of questions in the survey were about a multitude of topics which could be considered sensitive and therefore lead to social desirability bias. He hypothesised, in line with previous assumptions and evidence, that less socially desirable responding would be seen among respondents completing the web survey over the face-to-face interview - in other words, those who had to tell the interviewer their response were more likely to provide socially desirable responses than those that could input their answer in secrecy using the web module. The sample of respondents were students at a university in Belgium.

The behaviours and traits measured in the study and the hypothesised desirability of those things were as follows:

- School activities: being involved in more non-mandatory activities at school is more desirable.
- School integration: reporting being more socially integrated at school is more desirable.
- Utilitarian individualism: this is a belief that individuals should aim for personal success (self-interest) rather than care for the needs of others. Scoring highly on a utilitarian individualism scale could be seen as socially undesirable.
- Social dominance orientation: those high on this scale have a tendency to view social groups in a ranked manner; they perceive some groups to be 'better' than others. Scoring highly on a social dominance orientation scale could be seen as socially undesirable.
- General happiness, health and social satisfaction: three general items were included which looked at satisfaction across these domains. Socially desirable responses would be those that are more positive - for example, reporting being 'very satisfied' or 'rather satisfied', in 'very good' health, and so on.
- Number of friends: the higher the number of friends, the more socially desirable.

The experiment found, as expected, that most of the behaviours and traits examined were affected by social desirability bias, with a higher proportion of socially desirable answers recorded in the face-to-face interviews than in the web surveys. Respondents interviewed face-to-face reported a higher number of non-mandatory school activities, higher levels of social integration in school, lower scores on the social dominance

(Continued)

orientation scale, and higher scores on the general happiness, health and social satisfaction questions. However, it should be noted that significant differences were not found for the utilitarian individualism scale, nor in the reported number of friends.

This shows that social desirability bias can be a problem with face-to-face surveys when sensitive topics are covered, although not necessarily for all questions a researcher considers sensitive.

Variability in interviewer behaviour or characteristics

Human interviewers can impact responses to survey questions in a number of ways. They may not stick to the survey script, meaning that the same questions are asked differently to different respondents, resulting in different responses. For example, interviewers may provide different definitions or explanations of concepts to respondents, impacting the participant's response and potentially therefore measurement. In addition, characteristics about the interviewer themselves, such as gender or race, may lead to respondents answering questions differently than they might if interviewed by someone with different personal characteristics. Harling and colleagues (2018) explored the issues of interviewer variability in the context of a longitudinal study in South Africa that attempted to collect social network data.

Research spotlight

Harling, G. et al. (2018) 'Interviewer-driven variability in social network reporting: Results from Health and Aging in Africa: A Longitudinal Study of an INDEPTH community (HAALSI) in South Africa'

The Health and Aging in Africa: A Longitudinal Study of an INDEPTH community (HAALSI), is a longitudinal study of people aged 40 years and older in South Africa. One of the modules of the questionnaire implemented at the baseline wave of the study intended to capture social network information using face-to-face CAPI interviews. Specifically, the questionnaire asked: 'Please tell me the names of 6 adults with whom you have been in communication either in person or by phone or by internet in the past 6 months, starting with the person who is most important to you for any reason.' After listing the people, follow-up questions were then asked to determine some additional information about these people and the respondent's relationship with them.

During data collection, it was noticed that the number of people who were enlisted for this question dropped over time. It was also noted that there was interviewer variation in the average number of people listed - female interviewers, younger interviewers and those who conducted a greater share of interviews were more likely to elicit more names from respondents. However, for all interviewers, the number of names they elicited via this question dropped over time.

At some point into fieldwork, the field management team started conducting weekly meetings with interviewers, where the issue of declining numbers of names being provided for the social network question was discussed. At this point, there was a sharp rise in the average number of names given for this question.

Harling and colleagues consider many explanations for this pattern, but ultimately, they conclude that interviewers may have learnt that they were able to reduce the length of the survey by eliciting fewer names to the social network question, thus reducing the number of follow-up questions they were required to ask.

STUDY **PROFILE**

Health and Aging in Africa: A Longitudinal Study of an INDEPTH Community in South Africa (HAALSI)

Established: 2014.

Country: South Africa.

Sampling unit: individuals.

Sample size at base: 5,059 individuals.

Frequency of interviews: irregular; 2014-15, 2018, 2021.

Participants: men and women aged 40+.

Topics covered: physical and cognitive functioning, lifestyle risk factors, household income and expenditure, depression and mental health, social networks and family composition, HIV infection, cardiometabolic disease.

Methods of data collection: face-to-face interviews, telephone interviews.

Innovative features: biomarker collection.

Data availability: data are available to the research community via the Harvard Dataverse, Inter-university Consortium for Political and Social Research (ICPSR) and INDEPTH data repository.

More information: https://haalsi.org/

Higher item non-response to sensitive questions

Some survey questions may be considered sensitive by respondents, such as those asking about sexuality, income or risky behaviour, for example. When faced with an interviewer, respondents may feel uncomfortable answering sensitive questions, so decline to provide an answer at all, increasing item non-response. Item non-response may also not occur at random. It may be that some respondents are more likely to refuse to answer certain questions, therefore biasing results if this is not accounted for.

For example, for income questions, those at the lower end of the income spectrum may refuse to disclose their income to an interviewer. As such, estimates of average income of the population of interest may be higher than the true average income amount because of this non-response at one end of the spectrum (Frick and Grabka, 2010). However, in a longitudinal context, item non-response may pose less of an issue than with cross-sectional studies for two reasons:

1. It may be that as a study goes on and respondents participate over multiple waves, they build up a level of trust of the study and rapport with an interviewer (if they have been interviewed by the same interviewer on multiple occasions). This increased trust and rapport can lead to lower levels of item non-response. See Chapter 5 for a discussion on this topic.
2. In a longitudinal study, participants have often been participating for a long period of time and have already provided the study with large amounts of information. In the event that an item-non-response does occur in later waves, the information already provided at prior waves can be used to fill in missing responses with a 'best guess' estimate. This process is known as 'imputation'. Imputing data can make more cases available for analysis and can also reduce bias in estimates. See Chapter 4 for more information on imputation specifically and handling missing data more generally. The Research Spotlight by Frick and Grabka (2010) also highlights the benefits of imputation in a longitudinal context.

Research spotlight

Frick, J.R. and Grabka, M.M. (2010) 'Item nonresponse and imputation of annual labor income in panel surveys from a cross national perspective'

Frick and Grabka set out to look at item non-response and subsequent imputation to labour income questions in three longitudinal studies: the British Household Panel Study (BHPS), the German Socio-Economic Panel (SOEP) and the Household, Income and Labour Dynamics in Australia Survey (HILDA). For all three studies, for the years used in the analysis, interviews were conducted primarily face-to-face (the exception being for SOEP, where telephone interviews were used when a face-to-face interview could not be achieved).

The researchers found the level of item non-response to income questions in each study to be very similar. For SOEP across the period looked at in the research (1992-2004) the item non-response rate for the income question was about 14 per cent. For BHPS across 1991-2004, this figure was 15 per cent and for HILDA across 2001-5, it was 16 per cent.

Frick and Grabka then used longitudinal imputation techniques to impute missing values for income across all studies, which showed that because item non-response was not random, without imputation, the distribution of income was biased. Longitudinal data allowed the researchers to see a much more accurate picture of income in all three studies than would have been possible with a cross-sectional dataset.

STUDY **PROFILE**

Household, Income and Labour Dynamics in Australia Survey (HILDA)

Established: 2001.

Country: Australia.

Sampling unit: households.

Sample size at base: 19,914 individuals.

Frequency of interviews: annual.

Participants: all adults (16+) resident in the sampled household.

Topics covered: economic and personal well-being, labour market dynamics, family life.

Methods of data collection: face-to-face and telephone interviews.

Data availability: data are available to the research community via the National Centre for Longitudinal Data Dataverse.

More information: https://melbourneinstitute.unimelb.edu.au/hilda

Acquiescence bias

Acquiescence bias describes the tendency of some respondents to agree with statements or provide responses that are positive (rather than negative), introducing bias into data. This is obviously particularly problematic for scales that use an agree–disagree format. Acquiescent responding is most likely to occur in interviewer-administered survey modes, as opposed to self-administered ones

Telephone interviews

Telephone interviews are another popular choice for longitudinal surveys, particularly in countries where the geographic spread of respondents is large.

Benefits of using telephone interviews

Telephone interviewing can provide some benefits over other interview modes.

Cost

Unlike having to send interviewers to respondents' houses in face-to-face surveys, telephone interviewers can work in a central location, cutting out the costs associated with interviewer travel. The use of telephone interviews can be particularly efficient when respondents are spread over vast geographic areas.

Interviewer rapport

As with face-to-face surveys, telephone surveys can allow the interviewer to build up some rapport with the respondent, encouraging them to complete the questionnaire.

Interviewer support

Again, as with face-to-face modes, the use of a real person as an interviewer allows them to support the respondent in the completion of the questionnaire, clarifying concepts and helping the respondent with any issues they have answering the questionnaire.

Disadvantages of using telephone interviews

Telephone surveys may also have a number of drawbacks.

Social desirability bias

As telephone interviews use a real person, albeit over the telephone rather than face-to-face, social desirability bias may still occur.

Acquiescence bias

The tendency of respondents to agree with statements or provide positive responses – acquiescence bias – can theoretically occur in interviews conducted by telephone as there is still an interviewer involved in survey administration.

Higher item non-response to sensitive questions

Again, because a real interviewer is used, respondents may not be comfortable or willing to answer questions about topics they feel are sensitive or personal in nature. As such, item non-response may be higher.

Recency effects

In audio modes of survey administration, such as the telephone, if respondents are presented with a long list of response options, they are more likely to select options towards the end of the list. A major theory as to why this may occur was proposed by Krosnick and Alwin in 1987 and relates to human memory. It is theorised that items heard later in a list are more likely to be still stored in working memory, replacing items that are heard earlier in a list. As such, these items are easier to retrieve and therefore report. This has been termed '**recency effects**'. One way to overcome recency effects is to randomise the order of presentation of response options so that different respondents hear the list of response options in different orders. Data users should check to see if this has been done and, if not, should be aware of this in their analysis.

Research spotlight

Krosnick, J.A. and Alwin, D.F. (1987) 'An evaluation of a cognitive theory of response order effects in survey measurement'

Krosnick and Alwin realised that there was a large body of research that showed that the order response options were presented to respondents impacted on the responses that were likely to be chosen, but noted little research into why that might be the case. As such, they drew on literature from psychology to propose a theory for why response order effects occur.

The theory began with human memory - specifically, how memories are formed. For recency effects in particular, they noted that if lists of items are read aloud, there isn't time for the brain to process each option in depth. Each new item read from a list stops the processing of the items before it. As such, items at the end of the list are more likely to be subject to deeper processing. This may make them more attractive responses for respondents. In addition, items presented later in the list are more likely to still be retained in short-term memory, making them more easily accessible for respondents. Krosnick and Alwin theorised from this that recency effects may be more likely to occur in respondents who have problems with memory or who are paying less attention to the interviewer who is reading the response options.

They also formulated an argument for primacy effects, which is where respondents are likely to choose a response towards the top, rather than the bottom of a list. This most often occurs in visual modes of survey data collection, such as self-completion questionnaires on paper, on the interviewer's tablet computer or on the web. Again, the theory considers human processing of information and memory formation. When responses are presented visually, deeper cognitive processing is afforded to items at the top of a list. As a respondent goes down the list, their memory becomes crowded with items towards the top of the list. Therefore, deep processing of later items does not occur, making the selection of earlier items more likely. In addition, early items provide the respondent with a framework by which they judge later items. As the framework is then based around these early items, the respondent may consider them more important and end up being more likely to select them.

Researchers should be aware of the possibility of response order effects if they are analysing data obtained using questions with long lists of response options.

Variations on telephone interviews

The development of technology has led to a variation on the traditional telephone survey in the form of Interactive Voice Recognition (IVR). This is where the interview is done using the telephone, but rather than a live interviewer, an automated system is used. The system reads out a question to the respondent, usually using a text-to-speech program. Participants can then record their answer either by speaking or by pressing buttons on their phone's keypad, triggering the next question. This method can overcome some of the problems with using real interviewers on the telephone, including social desirability bias (Tourangeau et al., 2002) and item non-response to sensitive questions.

Research spotlight

Tourangeau, R., Steiger, D.M. and Wilson, D. (2002) 'Self-administered questions by telephone: Evaluating interactive voice response'

Tourangeau, Steiger and Wilson set out to evaluate how data obtained from IVR interviews compared with that obtained using a traditional telephone survey, as well as with a mail survey. They conducted a number of experiments to investigate response rates and data quality.

The study came to two main conclusions about IVR, one positive and one negative. First, IVR seemed to increase the honesty of respondents when compared with CATI. When asked satisfaction questions, the average level of satisfaction reported by IVR respondents was lower than that reported to telephone interviewers. In addition, the IVR responses were more highly correlated with other related questions than for telephone responses, further indicating honesty.

However, the experiments also showed that IVR tended to lead to more **break-offs** - that is, far more respondents started the questionnaire and then stopped part-way through when using IVR when compared with telephone interviews. The authors hypothesise that it is easier for a reluctant respondent to stop a questionnaire half-way through when they don't have to tell a live interviewer they want to stop and can instead just hang up the phone. They recommend keeping an IVR interview very short to minimise the volume of break-offs experienced.

This research shows that IVR has potential in some situations to collect high-quality data, but like all other methods, it also has its downsides.

CONCLUSIONS

Verbal methods of interviewing provide many benefits. The presence of interviewers can increase response rates as well as respondent cooperation. However, there are also drawbacks, including social desirability bias, acquiescence bias and higher reluctance to respond to sensitive questions. As well as this, the variability in interviewers, their characteristics and techniques, could influence responses. For telephone interviews in particular, recency effects could be an issue. The development of new technology has led to innovation in verbal methods of interviewing, providing computer-assisted methods as well as telephone methods that don't require a human interviewer – namely, IVR. Researchers conducting studies should be aware of the advantages and disadvantages of each data-collection method and choose the best fit for their study.

Chapter 10 will explore the issues covered in this chapter in combination with other survey design choices in the longitudinal context.

Key learning points

- The method by which survey data is collected is known as the 'mode'.
- Face-to-face interviews have traditionally been the 'mode of choice' for surveys.
- Face-to-face interviews with information collected electronically, rather than on paper, have a number of benefits:
    - questionnaire routing;
    - data quality checks;
    - feeding forward of historical information;
    - ease of data processing.
- There are a number of benefits of using face-to-face interviews over other methods:
    - increased response rates;
    - interviewer rapport;
    - interviewer support.
- There are drawbacks of using face-to-face interviews over other methods:
    - social desirability bias;
    - variation in interviewers;
    - higher item non-response to sensitive questions;
    - acquiescence bias.
- Telephone interviews provide some advantages over other modes:
    - cost;
    - interviewer rapport;
    - interviewer support.
- Telephone interviews have potential flaws when compared with other interviewing methods:
    - social desirability bias;
    - variation in interviewers;

(Continued)

 - higher item non-response to sensitive questions;
 - recency effects.
- Interactive Voice Response is a variation on the traditional telephone survey, where a computer reads the questions to the respondent over the telephone and the participant responds either verbally or by pressing numbers on their telephone keypad.

Check your understanding

1. Describe the advantages of using computerised face-to-face interviewing (CAPI) over the paper-based, face-to-face method.
2. What are the advantages of using face-to-face interviews over other modes of data collection?
3. What are the disadvantages of telephone interviewing?
4. Why might IVR be a good alternative to telephone interviewing?

WANT TO FIND OUT MORE?

The resources below are great sources of additional information on the content covered in this section.

For an overview of face-to-face interviewing methodology and considerations:

Loosveldt, G. (2008) 'Face-to-face interviews', in de Leeuw, E., Hox, J.J. and Dillman, D.A. (eds) *International Handbook of Survey Methodology*. New York: Psychology Press.

For an overview of telephone interviewing methodology and considerations:

Steeh, C. (2008) 'Telephone surveys', in de Leeuw, E., Hox, J.J. and Dillman, D.A. (eds) *International Handbook of Survey Methodology*. New York: Psychology Press.

9

MODE OF DATA COLLECTION: VISUAL MODES

OVERVIEW OF CONTENT

This chapter will provide you with an overview of the main visual modes of data collection – namely, self-completion questionnaires, either administered by mail or as part of an interviewer visit, and web surveys. It will explain the advantages and disadvantages of each method.

Some of the advantages and disadvantages pertinent to longitudinal studies that are introduced in this chapter will be expanded on further in separate chapters in this book, and this is signposted where necessary. Chapter 10, on the implications of design choices for longitudinal studies, will also explore some of these issues further.

Learning outcomes

After you have read this chapter, you will be able to:

- understand why different data-collection modes are used in longitudinal research;
- explain the benefits of using computerised rather than paper-based data collection;
- describe the benefits of carrying out research using visual data-collection modes;
- describe the drawbacks of visual modes.

VISUAL DATA-COLLECTION MODES

As well as the verbal modes discussed in Chapter 8, there are survey modes that are primarily visual. Originally, this would have been self-completion questionnaires completed on paper. This could be a mail survey that is sent to the respondent in the post and is posted back when completed. Alternatively, a paper self-completion could be part of an interviewer face-to-face visit, where the respondent completes a set of questions in private (usually the more sensitive questions).

As technology developed, self-completion questionnaires in the home became available electronically, so rather than completing a paper questionnaire, respondents could use the interviewer's electronic device to complete the questions.

The other main visual mode of survey administration is web questionnaires, a special case of a self-completion questionnaire. These are becoming increasingly common, in part due to the fact that large proportions of many populations now have access to internet-enabled devices.

Visual modes, like any other, offer their own advantages and disadvantages, particularly in the context of a longitudinal study.

Self-administered questionnaires

Self-administered questionnaires, or self-completion questionnaires, are a common data-collection method used in longitudinal surveys. Previously, these questionnaires were exclusively paper questionnaires, but more recently with advances in technology, computerised self-completions ('computer-assisted self-completion interviews', or CASI) have become more common.

CASI questionnaires offer benefits over their paper counterparts. These benefits are the same as CAPI offers over paper-based interviewer-administered questionnaires. More detail can be found in Chapter 8, but in brief:

1. It allows for complex questionnaire routing. Questions can be tailored based on responses to previous questions. While this is possible on paper, it is easier for respondents using CASI as they don't have to work out the correct routing themselves.
2. Data quality checks can be implemented. The questionnaire can be programmed to spot inconsistent or unlikely responses and flag to the respondent the potential problem, encouraging them to either confirm their response or edit any incorrect information.
3. Historical information can be 'fed forward'. In the context of a longitudinal survey, responses that respondents have given in previous interviews can be automatically fed into a future survey in order to reduce the questionnaire length and avoid asking unnecessary or irrelevant questions, or to reduce the recall burden on the respondent.

4. Data processing is easier. Rather than having to manually enter the paper questionnaire responses into a computer-based or punch-card system, the data are already in an electronic format, ready for processing and use. This removes the possibility of error being introduced by incorrect responses being transferred from paper to an electronic system.

Benefits of using self-administered questionnaires

Self-administered questionnaires can offer benefits over using an interviewer-administered mode.

Increased reporting of sensitive behaviours, information and attitudes

The reasons for increased reporting of sensitive behaviours, information and attitudes are twofold. First, because there isn't a person present who the respondent has to report sensitive information to, they may feel comfortable providing information about sensitive topics, such as their income or risky behaviours. This reduces item non-response. Second, social desirability bias is less of a problem. Social desirability bias is the tendency of some respondents to respond to a question in a way that they feel is socially acceptable or desirable, even when the response isn't accurate. This can lead to underreporting of attitudes or behaviours that are seen as negative or undesirable, and overreporting of desirable behaviours and attitudes. Using data from one of the UK birth cohorts, the National Child Development Study (NCDS), Goodman and colleagues (2022) investigated the impact of mode on the reporting of sensitive information.

Research spotlight

Goodman, A. et al. (2022) 'The impact of using the Web in a mixed-mode follow-up of a longitudinal birth cohort study: Evidence from the National Child Development Study'

The National Child Development Study is a longitudinal cohort study in Great Britain, following people born in a particular week in 1958. There have been multiple waves of data collection, predominantly collected face-to-face. In the study's eleventh wave, when participants were aged 55, a sequential mixed-mode design was introduced for the first time. Most participants were first invited to complete the study online and then those who did not were invited to participate via the telephone. However,

(Continued)

a small subset of respondents were allocated to a telephone-only mode. This gave Goodman and colleagues the opportunity to investigate mode effects in the context of a long-running longitudinal study.

They found that, as theories suggested, those respondents completing the survey over the telephone were more likely to provide more desirable responses. For example, those who were interviewed on the telephone were more likely to self-report being in better health and less likely to provide responses to health questions which led to them being classified as having a long-standing health issue or being disabled. The telephone group gave lower numbers when asked about the number of units of alcohol they had consumed over the previous seven days. They also responded more positively to a range of measures capturing different facets of well-being and reported participating in a higher level of different leisure activities.

This research shows that even in the context of a longitudinal study that respondents have spent many years participating in, mode effects can still be present across a range of different survey questions.

Standardisation of the survey

Self-administered surveys are more standardised than interviewer-administered surveys because the 'human factor' of the interviewer is removed. The way that interviewers ask questions, the additional information they provide respondents and even their personal characteristics can affect responses participants give (see Chapter 8 for more information on the ways that interviewers can affect participant responses). Using non-interviewer-administered modes of data collection removes the possibility that interviewer effects will introduce bias into the data.

There are additional benefits of using mail or online surveys over those administered by an interviewer in the household.

Convenience for the respondent

Another benefit of a self-administered survey is that respondents can complete the questionnaire at a time convenient to them. Rather than feeling rushed to complete the questionnaire, the respondent may spend more time thinking about their responses or even consulting their own records, such as wage slips, to provide precise answers. This could offer benefits in terms of accuracy and therefore data quality.

Disadvantages of using self-administered questionnaires

Alongside the advantages of using a self-administered survey mode, there are some drawbacks.

Primacy effects

In visual modes of survey administration, like paper or computerised self-completion questionnaires, if respondents are presented with a long list of response options, they are likely to select an option higher up in the list and less likely to select one towards the bottom of the list. This is known as a primacy effect. There are a few theories on why this might occur.

It may be because the items earlier on in the list are more effectively stored in long-term memory, so are more likely to be retrieved. See Chapter 8 for a summary of a study by Krosnick and Alwin that explores theories for how human processing and memory can create response order effects (Krosnick and Alwin, 1987).

The respondent may be going down the list looking for the first acceptable answer they see and not read the list in full. This behaviour has been described as 'satisficing' – for some respondents and some questions, providing an accurate answer can be cognitively challenging for a number of reasons. Instead of expending the cognitive effort to retrieve the optimal answer, respondents may instead provide an answer that they think will be seen as acceptable, but is not necessarily optimal or correct. Satisficing can be seen in a number of different response strategies, including those that cause primacy effects. When faced with a long list of response options, rather than reading each item in turn and then making a judgement about which best fits their own opinion or behaviour, respondents may work their way down the list looking for the first answer they deem to be acceptable, causing primacy effects (Krosnick, 1991).

One way to overcome primacy effects is to randomise the order of presentation of response options. Data users should check to see if this has been done and, if not, should be aware of this in their analysis.

Lack of an interviewer available to support completion

If the respondent gets stuck with the survey – for example, if they don't understand a question – interviewer support will not be available.

Variations on CASI formats

As well as the traditional CASI mode, where respondents view the survey on the interviewer's computer and respond themselves, a variation called audio-CASI (A-CASI) has been developed. This can be implemented in two ways. Either the questions appear on the screen and they are simultaneously read out to the respondent by the computer, or the computer reads the questions with no accompanying text on-screen. This mode is particularly useful for the visually impaired and those with low literacy levels who may struggle to read the questionnaire themselves. This retains the benefits of not having an interviewer involved, so should reduce the likelihood of social desirability bias occurring as well as keep the questionnaire standardised. There is evidence to suggest that the differences between responses obtained using CASI as compared with A-CASI are minimal (Couper et al., 2003), which is reassuring for studies that give respondents the choice of which method they wish to use.

Research spotlight

Couper, M.P. et al. (2003) 'Understanding the effects of audio-Casi on self-reports of sensitive behavior'

Couper and colleagues set out to explicitly compare responses to traditional CASI questions with those obtained using A-CASI, recognising that very little research on this topic had been done at that time. They knew that self-administration offered advantages over interviewer-administered survey methods, but hypothesised that the presence of a third party in the room may affect responses to CASI and A-CASI differently. Specifically, where a third person is present and is able to see the screen the respondent is using while completing a CASI questionnaire, less accurate and more socially desirable responses will be obtained compared to when the respondent is using A-CASI, set up with no accompanying text. Further to this, they also thought that when there was no third party present, CASI would yield more accurate answers and less socially desirable responses than A-CASI, because A-CASI introduces an 'interviewer', albeit virtual.

To test these hypotheses, Couper and colleagues implemented an experiment. What they found was contrary to expectation. Reporting of sensitive behaviour was the same across CASI and A-CASI, generally regardless of whether or not there was a third party in the room who was able to see the computer screen. They conclude that variations on different types of CASI administration have little impact on the data obtained from sensitive questions.

These findings are reassuring for those studies that use a mix of CASI and A-CASI, in the sense that responses across the two methods should be comparable.

Online surveys

With the development of the internet and the proliferation of internet-enabled device use across developed countries in particular, web surveys are becoming an increasingly popular choice. They offer a number of benefits over other methods of data collection, but come with their own set of drawbacks, too.

Benefits of using online surveys

Online surveys offer a number of advantages over other modes.

Flexibility for the respondent

The survey can be completed at any time of day and in any place convenient for the participant. Rather than feeling pressured to complete the questionnaire, the respondent may spend more time thinking about their responses and even consulting their own records, such as wage slips or doctors' records, to provide precise answers. This could offer benefits in terms of increased data quality through accuracy.

Increased reporting of sensitive behaviours, information and attitudes

As with CASI or paper self-completion questionnaires, respondents may feel more comfortable reporting on private or sensitive behaviours and attitudes because there is no human interviewer present. This may reduce social desirability bias and item non-response.

Standardisation of the survey

Again, like other self-completion surveys, the lack of human interviewer means that the survey is administered in a more standardised way. The way that interviewers ask questions, the additional information they provide respondents, and even their personal characteristics, can affect the responses that participants give (see Chapter 8 for more information on the ways that interviewers can affect participant responses).

Data quality checks can be implemented

Checks that flag unlikely or impossible responses can be built into a web survey, increasing data quality. An additional quality factor that can be assessed is the speed with which the respondent completes the survey. It is generally accepted that respondents who are answering a web survey extremely quickly (faster than the questions can be read in full by most people) are providing responses of low quality through the mechanism of satisficing (for more information on satisficing, see 'Disadvantages of using self-administered surveys' in this chapter). A web survey can also be tailored to try to prevent this behaviour in order to increase data quality via programming it to warn the respondent that they are completing the questions too quickly, and advise them that they should slow down and take time to read the questions properly. Conrad and colleagues (2017) explore the impact of implementing this warning technique in a number of online surveys.

Research spotlight

Conrad, F.G., Couper, M.P., Tourangeau, R. and Zhang, C. (2017) 'Reducing speeding in web surveys by providing immediate feedback'

Conrad and colleagues recognised that respondents who answer web surveys extremely quickly were likely to be satisficing, providing responses of questionable accuracy and quality. As such, they designed an experiment to see whether they could reduce speeding, through the use of a prompt that appeared on-screen when respondents were deemed to be answering too quickly, and evaluated the impact of the prompt on later respondent behaviour. The experiment was implemented across six different web surveys.

Their headline finding was that the use of the prompt reduced speeding during later parts of the questionnaire, suggesting that respondents at least read the message and altered their behaviour accordingly. The prompt was effective for respondents who were completing the first wave of a longitudinal study and those who had taken part previously, for those who were caught speeding early and late in the questionnaire, and for those who saw the prompt just once, after the first time they were speeding, and for participants who saw the prompt every time they were deemed to be speeding.

One concern of introducing the prompt was that it would be seen as annoying by respondents and they would simply stop with the online questionnaire, known as a 'break-off'. This did not materialise, which is reassuring for studies that use speeding prompts.

The researchers also found that for one of the experiments, **straightlining** (or non-differentiation) was reduced. Straightlining is a type of satisficing, where respondents faced with a grid of questions select the same response for all items in the grid without differentiating between their responses. Therefore, for some respondents at least, the speeding prompt increased data quality.

The results suggest that implementing a technique to reduce speeding in web surveys could have a positive impact on data quality and could work in a longitudinal context.

Breaking the survey into manageable blocks

The questionnaire can be programmed so that it can be stopped and restarted multiple times. By the respondent breaking down the survey into blocks that are convenient to them, they may feel less burdened and be more likely to ultimately complete the entire survey, reducing break-offs and increasing response rates. Alternatively, the researcher is also able to break the questionnaire into smaller parts, or module, and send them to respondents periodically, with a view of reducing the burden placed on a respondent at a single point in time. Toepoel and Lugtig (2022) investigated the effect of modularising an online survey in the context of the Longitudinal Internet Study for the Social Sciences (LISS) Panel in the Netherlands.

Research spotlight

Toepoel, V. and Lugtig, P. (2022) 'Modularization in an era of mobile web: Investigating the effects of cutting a survey into smaller pieces on data quality'

Mobile phones are increasingly being used by respondents to complete online surveys, and with this comes the need for surveys to be shorter to encourage smartphone users to complete the whole survey. Toepoel and Lugtig sought to investigate the impact of breaking up longer online surveys into chunks, or modules, and periodically sending respondents modules to complete on different facets of response and data quality.

Using the Longitudinal Internet Study for the Social Sciences (LISS) Panel in the Netherlands, they embedded an experiment that randomly assigned respondents to receive a particular survey either in its entirety, in three parts or in ten parts, where the modularised version was sent at regular intervals over the course of a month.

They found that when respondents received the shorter survey modules, the rate of respondents starting the survey was higher than when the survey was sent out in its long, non-modular form, but also that break-off rates were here. However, in terms of data quality, item non-response is lower in the modularised conditions and instances of satisficing are reduced, both leading to higher data quality.

These findings show that in a longitudinal context, breaking down an online survey into smaller chunks, or modules, may offer benefits, particularly for data quality.

STUDY PROFILE

Longitudinal Internet Studies for the Social Sciences Panel (LISS)

Established: 2007.

Country: Netherlands

Sampling unit: households.

Sample size at base: c. 4,500 households.

Frequency of interviews: monthly (plus core interview completed annually).

Participants: all adults (16+) resident in the sampled household.

Topics covered: wide ranging, as researchers can apply to include topics of their choice.

Methods of data collection: web surveys.

Innovative features: immigrant panel (2010-14).

Data availability: data are available to the research community via the LISS Data Archive.

More information: www.lissdata.nl/Home

Disadvantages of using online surveys

As well as the benefits of using online surveys, there are some disadvantages.

Respondent distraction

As respondents are able to complete the survey when and where they want, there is a risk that they will become distracted. If they are distracted, they will likely take longer to complete the survey and may not be providing the most accurate answers they can, leading to error in the data. However, recent evidence on this topic, provided by Ansolabehere and Schaffner (2015), suggests that respondent distraction during web survey completion may not be as bad for data quality as once thought.

Research spotlight

Ansolabehere, S. and Schaffner, B.F. (2015) 'Distractions: The incidence and consequences of interruptions for survey respondents'

The authors set out to investigate just how bad respondent distraction during web surveys was for data quality. They looked at four web surveys, some cross-sectional and some panel, all with a political focus. Respondents were all asked at the end of the survey to report whether they had done anything else while completing the survey and were provided with a list of options to choose from, such as 'sent a text', 'do a chore' and 'watch television'.

They found that over half the respondents they surveyed reported distraction during the 30-minute survey. The most common reasons given were watching television and speaking with another adult. They also found that respondents who took the survey on their smartphone were more likely to report a distraction compared with those using desktops, laptops and tablets. With the increase in smartphone ownership, and in resultant surveys using smartphones, this could pose a problem.

Unsurprisingly, respondents who reported distractions took longer to complete the survey. However, the results on survey quality were reassuring. The authors looked at two different measures of quality. First, consistency in responses and second, responses to factual questions. There was no evidence in differences on these metrics between respondents who reported being distracted and those who did not.

This research provides reassuring evidence that distraction during a web survey may not be as bad for data quality as previously thought. However, it is still an issue that survey designers and data users should be aware of.

Lack of interviewer involvement

While interviewers bring some disadvantages to survey administration, they can also be key in motivating respondents to complete the survey. With no interviewers involved with web surveys, respondents may be less encouraged to complete the survey. This in turn is likely to decrease response rates. Heerwegh and Loosveldt (2008) look at response rates in the context of web versus face-to-face surveys.

Research spotlight

Heerwegh, D. and Loosveldt, G. (2008) 'Face-to-face versus web surveying in a high-internet-coverage population: Differences in response quality'

In order to assess response rates to a web survey versus a face-to-face interview, Heerwegh and Loosveldt implemented a split ballot experiment in a survey in a university in Belgium. They randomly assigned some sample members to complete a face-to-face interview and some to complete the equivalent questionnaire online.

The differences in response rate were quite striking. Of the web sample, 62.9 per cent logged in to the survey. However, 16.6 per cent stopped part-way through, leaving 52.5 per cent completing it. For the face-to-face sample, on the other hand, 92.2 per cent responded.

However, it should be noted that the sample used for this study were first-year students at a university. It may be that this finding, at least a difference as stark as this, may not be found in all populations.

However, in a longitudinal context, it may be that differences in response rates are not as much as a challenge for cross-sectional surveys. Given that respondents have often been participating in longitudinal studies for some time, they may feel committed to the study, and so are likely to participate regardless of the mode that they have been asked to take part in, even when an interviewer is not present. In addition, many longitudinal studies are transitioning to a mixed-mode approach, whereby respondents are initially asked to participate online, then non-responders are followed up using other methods, often telephone or face-to-face (see Chapter 10 for more information on mixed-mode approaches). Next Steps, a longitudinal study in the UK, has successfully implemented this approach.

STUDY PROFILE

Next Steps (previously known as the Longitudinal Study of Young People in England - LSYPE)

Established: 2004.

Country: England.

Sampling unit: individuals.

Sample size at base: 15,770.

Frequency of interviews: annually from 2004 to 2010, then 2015.

Participants: a sample of young people who were in Year 9 in English state and independent schools and pupil referral units in February 2004.

Topics covered: initially education-focused, but expanded to include health, well-being, finances, employment, social participation and attitudes.

Methods of data collection: face-to-face, telephone and web.

Innovative features: data linkage.

Data availability: data are available to the research community via the UK Data Archive.

More information: https://cls.ucl.ac.uk/cls-studies/next-steps/

Primacy effects

Due to the survey being visual, primacy effects may be seen for questions that have more than a handful of response options. See 'Disadvantages of using self-administered surveys' in this chapter for more information on why primacy effects may occur. Studies have shown that primacy effects may be an issue for web surveys, particularly for certain groups of respondents. Malhotra (2008) investigates primacy effects in web surveys specifically.

Research spotlight

Malhotra, N. (2008) 'Completion time and response order effects in web surveys'

Malhotra set out to investigate whether primacy effects really were a problem in web surveys, theorising that satisficing may be more of a problem in an online survey where an interviewer wasn't present, manifesting itself as a primacy effect. He recruited a random sample of adults in the US to explore this.

He embedded a number of attitudinal questions with either four- or five-point response scales in the survey. Half the respondents received the response options in one order and the other half saw them in the reverse order. This enables a primacy effect to be seen if there is one.

Malhotra found that respondents with low education and who completed the survey quickly were likely to show a primacy effect. The effect decreases for respondents with low education the longer they spend completing the survey. The same pattern was not seen for respondents who were highly educated.

He concluded that design features of web surveys could be implemented to reduce the likelihood of primacy effects biasing the data, including changing the order of responses when they were presented to respondents.

Coverage errors

While a large and increasing number of people have access to internet-enabled devices which they could use to take a web survey, a proportion of people do not. It is also likely that those who do not are different in some way to those who do. As such, if a survey is only available as a web survey, there is a risk of introducing bias through not including those who do not have access to the internet, known as **coverage error** or coverage bias.

One way to overcome the issue of respondents who do not have access to the internet is to provide the technology they need to respond to web surveys. This has been done successfully by the LISS panel in the Netherlands. The LISS sample is a representative sample of all households in the Netherlands, drawn from a population register. Households who did not have the technology needed to complete the web surveys were provided with a computer and an internet connection. In this way, the online panel retains the advantage of being a representative sample, successfully collecting longitudinal data via web surveys.

Variations on online formats

The fast-paced development of technology has enabled the development of different variations on web surveys. These innovations are particularly pertinent due to the rise in smartphone ownership, offering a new way to connect with many respondents.

Apps are now available to collect questionnaire data. The respondent can download a survey app to their smartphone and then the study can push surveys to the app as frequently as they wish, as well as using the app notifications to send reminders to complete the survey. A benefit of using an app is that, unlike a traditional web survey, respondents do not need to be connected to the internet to complete the survey (only to download the survey in the first place and then to return the data).

Mobile phones also offer the option of SMS or messenger surveys. The respondent is sent a question-and-response options via a message, and they respond with their answer. Once a response is received, the next question is sent. This method retains the benefit of allowing the respondent to answer the survey at a time and place convenient to them, and also when it may feel less burdensome (as they aren't faced with an entire survey in one go). Messenger surveys can be conducted by human interviewers manually sending messages or by automated systems.

CONCLUSIONS

Visual methods of interviewing provide many benefits. The privacy of a self-completion or web interview can encourage respondents to provide more accurate and honest answers, particularly to sensitive items, through the reduction of social desirability bias. The lack of an interviewer present can reduce some of the variability in interviews introduced by the 'human factor'. Web surveys in particular may be seen as less burdensome by respondents, as they can complete them at a time of their choosing and over more than one period if they wish. However, there are also drawbacks. The lack of interviewer may reduce the likelihood of the respondent either starting or finishing the survey, decreasing response rates and increasing break-offs. Visual modes in particular are also prone to primacy effects. When using the web, coverage errors may be introduced if the entire sample does not have access to the internet and therefore cannot participate. Innovations in web surveys in particular have led to the development of new data-collection methods, particularly SMS and app surveys.

Key learning points

- The main visual modes of survey administration are self-completion, either on paper or computer-assisted, and the web.
- Self-completion questionnaires with information collected electronically, rather than on paper, have a number of benefits:
    - questionnaire routing;
    - data quality checks;
    - feeding forward of historical information;
    - ease of data processing.
- There are a number of benefits of using self-completion questionnaires over other methods:
    - increased reporting of sensitive information;
    - standardisation of the survey;
    - for mail surveys, respondents can complete the questionnaire at a time convenient to them.
- There are drawbacks of using self-completion questionnaires over other methods:
    - primacy effects;
    - lack of interviewer available to support completion.

- Developments in technology have allowed an audio version of the self-completion questionnaire, A-CASI, which can be useful for respondents with visual impairments or low literacy levels.
- Web surveys provide some advantages over other modes:
    - flexibility for the respondent;
    - increased reporting of sensitive information;
    - standardisation of the survey;
    - data quality checks, including checks for extremely fast completion;
    - the questionnaire can be programmed so that it can be stopped and restarted multiple times.
- Web surveys have potential flaws when compared with other interviewing methods:
    - respondent distraction;
    - lack of interviewer involvement;
    - primacy effects;
    - coverage errors.
- Advances in technology have created advanced web-based opportunities for data collection including apps and SMS surveys.

Check your understanding

1. Describe the advantages of using computerised self-completion questionnaires (CASI) over the paper-based, face-to-face method.
2. What are the advantages of using self-completion questionnaires over interviewer-administered data-collection methods?
3. What are the advantages of web surveys?
4. What are the disadvantages of web surveys?

WANT TO FIND OUT MORE?

The resources below are great sources of additional information on the content covered in this section.

For an overview of self-administered questionnaire methodologies and considerations:

De Leeuw, E.D. and Hox, J. J. (2008) 'Self-administered questionnaires: Mail surveys and other applications', in de Leeuw, E., Hox, J.J. and Dillman, D.A. (eds) *International Handbook of Survey Methodology*. New York: Psychology Press.

For a history and future look at online surveys:

Evans, J.R. and Mathur, A. (2018) 'The value of online surveys: A look back and a look ahead', *Internet Research*, 28 (4): 854–87.

10

MIXED-MODE STUDIES IN THE LONGITUDINAL CONTEXT

OVERVIEW OF CONTENT

This chapter will introduce you to some of the implications of different mode choices in the context of longitudinal studies. Specifically, we will look at what can happen when mode is altered between, or even within, waves of a longitudinal study. This builds on what we have discussed in Chapters 8 and 9, which looked at mode choices in isolation from one another.

This chapter will cover three key areas: non-response and attrition, bias, and measurement, outlining how mixed-mode approaches can be both positive and negative for each of these things.

Learning outcomes

After you have read this chapter, you will be able to:

- understand what mixed-mode study designs are in a longitudinal context;
- describe the pros and cons of using a mixed-mode design for a longitudinal study;

(Continued)

- understand the impact of mixed-mode designs on non-response and attrition;
- understand the impact of mixed-mode designs on bias;
- understand the impact of mixed-mode designs on measurement.

WHAT ARE THE IMPLICATIONS OF MODE CHOICES FOR LONGITUDINAL STUDIES?

As we have learned in previous chapters, a number of design decisions must be made when creating a longitudinal study or specific waves of a study. These design choices centre on two different aspects of creation: 1) The format that each question takes; 2) The mode in which to survey respondents.

This chapter will focus on survey mode decisions in a longitudinal context, specifically what can happen when mode is altered between, or even within, waves of a longitudinal study.

Survey mode decisions in a longitudinal context

To remind ourselves of the content of Chapters 8 and 9, Figure 10.1 shows an overview of the methodological pros and cons of each main method of data collection.

Method	Pros	Cons
Face-to-face (CAPI) interview	+ interviewer available to clarify things the respondent has problems with + interviewer present to build a rapport with the respondent and encourage completion	– possibility of acquiescence bias – possibility of socially desirable responding – likely increase item non-response for sensitive questions – hard to completely standardise because of the presence of a human interviewer who can go 'off script'
Self-completion questionnaire	+ likely to increase honest reporting for sensitive questions	– primacy effects more likely
Telephone interview	+ interviewer available to clarify things the respondent has problems with	– possibility of acquiescence bias – possibility of socially desirable responding – likely increase item non-response for sensitive questions – recency effects more likely
Web survey	+ can be done by the respondent in their own time + likely to increase honest reporting for sensitive questions	– respondents may get distracted when completing the survey and as such concentrate less – lack of interviewer to encourage completion – primacy effects more likely

Figure 10.1 An overview of the methodological pros and cons of each main method of data collection

It is apparent from Figure 10.1 that there is no one mode that offers clear advantages over others and instead the choice is a trade-off. Decisions taken about which mode a study uses can be taken based on the pros and cons of each method, based on the type of questions being asked – for example, are they sensitive or not? – or on the profile of respondents – for example, will most of them have access to the internet or a telephone? Intertwined with this is often the issue of costs. A face-to-face survey, for example, can be very expensive to administer. The cost of employing interviewers to travel around visiting people to conduct the survey can be prohibitively expensive. An online survey, on the other hand, is often far cheaper to administer. There are no interviewer costs or travel costs, and instead the expense is limited to programming the survey and arranging distribution and completion reminders. A further consideration is the preferences of respondents. It may be that some respondents prefer to have an interviewer visit to complete the survey, whereas for others the flexibility of a telephone or online survey is better.

When the mode of interview remains stable across waves of a longitudinal study and is also the same within each wave, there are few implications for the resultant data – beyond those seen in the advantages or disadvantages for a single mode. However, if the mode is varied within or between waves, the impact on the data could be much greater. Varying mode within or between waves can come under the umbrella term of 'mixed-mode approaches'. The rest of this chapter will look at mixed-mode approaches and the impact they can have in a longitudinal context.

MIXED-MODE APPROACHES

Often, longitudinal studies employ a mix of modes in order to balance issues of cost, preference and access. While doing this can increase response rates and keep costs to an acceptable level, there can be consequences to the data of using a mixed-mode approach. This can occur when longitudinal studies use either different modes at different waves of the study or multiple modes within a single wave. When conducting analysis, researchers should be aware of the consequences to the data collected of using multiple modes by a longitudinal study.

Switching mode between waves

Studies will often choose to use different modes at different waves of the study. Again, this is often a cost issue. For example, if a study only has a finite budget (obviously, this is almost always the case) and they cannot afford to run an annual face-to-face survey, they may choose to make every other survey face-to-face and the waves between a different mode, such as online. This ensures regular data collection from respondents at a cost that is more affordable.

However, it is important to consider that often longitudinal studies wish to ask the same questions at multiple waves of a study. This allows an assessment of change or stability at an individual level, which is crucial to answering many longitudinal research questions. This might sound simple – why not just ask the same questions online as you would face-to-face? However, unfortunately that might not always work out as perfectly as you might hope.

As we will see later in this chapter, there can be consequences for the data of taking the approach of using different modes at different waves of a longitudinal study.

Using multiple modes within a wave

Some studies opt to use different modes within a single wave of a study. As alluded to previously, this can have real benefits for both response rates and cost. There are two different ways to achieve this. First, a sequential mixed mode approach could be used. This is where all respondents are asked to complete the study in one mode to start with. Then a different mode is used to follow up with non-responders. A common approach to a sequential mixed mode design is to encourage everyone to complete the survey online, as it is usually the cheapest option, then either telephone interviews or face-to-face visits (or both) are used to follow up with non-responders. This keeps costs down, but maximises the response rate.

The second approach is to offer all respondents all available modes of completion up front, allowing them to choose their preferred mode. This can encourage high response rates by allowing respondents to complete the survey in a way that suits them. If participants don't respond initially, targeting follow-ups using different modes – for example, face-to-face interviewers – can then be used to encourage completion.

However, as with switching modes between waves, there can be consequences of taking a mixed-mode approach. These will be discussed in the section below.

What are the implications of mixed-mode designs for longitudinal studies?

In a longitudinal context, it is important to understand which design decisions were taken in terms of mode when using the resultant data. The consequences of different choices can have an impact on the data produced by the study in a number of different ways. This could relate to response rates, attrition, bias or measurement. These issues are discussed in the following sections.

Response rates and attrition

One of the primary drivers of implementing a mixed-mode design is to increase response rates (with the additional benefit of potentially reducing cost). Offering respondents the opportunity to complete a survey in different modes may result in more people completing the survey overall, due to people being offered completion options which they prefer or are more comfortable with.

There has been research into the effects of using sequential mixed-mode approaches in a longitudinal study that has historically been carried out face-to-face only. Bianchi et al. (2017) examined response rates, attrition, achieved sample and costs when the UK Household Longitudinal Study switched from a face-to-face to mixed-mode approach.

Research spotlight

Bianchi, A., Biffignandi, S. and Lynn, P. (2017) 'Web-face-to-face mixed-mode design in a longitudinal survey: Effects on participation rates, sample composition, and costs'

Understanding Society, the UK Household Longitudinal Study, is an annual household panel study, capturing information about households as well as individuals in the UK. The study had historically solely used interviewers to capture information from participants face-to-face. However, the study team were keen to introduce different modes to the study, but recognised that it would be important to understand the impact of doing so on the resultant response rates, sample composition and cost. Understanding Society has an Innovation Panel, which in itself is a longitudinal study that was started in 2008 and used as a 'test bed' for the main study.

Using an experimental design, some Innovation Panel participants were assigned to get the usual face-to-face survey and some received an invitation to complete the survey using the web, with a follow-up face-to-face for those who did not complete the online survey. For both groups, a final mop-up of non-respondents was conducted using other modes, such as a telephone survey. Importantly, as well as looking at the response to the wave in which the experiment was conducted, the authors also considered the response at subsequent waves to assess whether there was an impact of different modes and mode sequences on attrition. It should be noted that Understanding Society is a household study, so there is interest in both household completion as well as completion of the survey by individuals residing in those households.

In terms of individual participation, the authors found no statistically significant differences in response rates at the first wave in which the experiment was implemented, nor at the subsequent two waves of data collection. However, at a household level, while the mixed-mode approach initially showed lower household response than the face-to-face only approach, by the third wave of data collection this was reversed, with higher household response in the mixed-mode approach. Looking at sample composition across the three waves of the experiment, the authors conclude that the differences between the two groups were minimal.

(Continued)

Finally, one of the major drivers of a mixed-mode approach is often the financial cost - and specifically, reducing the cost. The authors point out that the major cost saving should, in fact, be that using a non-face-to-face mode (web, in this instance) means that interviewers do not have to physically visit households (nor indeed be used at all with a web survey). For this study, cost savings were estimated to be around 15 per cent at the first wave, 8 per cent at the second wave and 11 per cent at the third wave. The authors note that the cost savings they calculate are likely not generalisable due to specific design parameters for the study, which probably do not apply to other studies.

The authors conclude that at least in the context of an ongoing panel study, a mixed-mode approach appears to be positive. There were no significant differences found in response rates across waves or the composition of participants, and sizeable cost savings were achieved.

However, switching modes across different waves of a longitudinal study could have the opposite impact for some groups of respondents. If a respondent is used to participating in the study in one mode, suddenly being offered a different mode may increase their reluctance to participate.

Bias

Bias refers to a systematic error that results in the over- or under-estimation of parameters in the data – that is to say, in the context of survey mode, certain types of people are more likely to respond to a survey in a particular mode. This type of bias is known as '**selection bias**' – the problem of people self-selecting into particular conditions, causing biases in the data. For example, if the survey is online, then people who have access to the internet and an appropriate device to complete the survey are more likely to participate. Similarly, those who are more comfortable and familiar with using the internet are more likely to respond. This can introduce bias, because those with no access to the internet or a device, or those who are uncomfortable with the relevant technology, are less likely to be represented in the data. These two different types of people are likely to be different not just in terms of their internet use and familiarity, but also on a whole range of other issues that a study might be interested in measuring.

For longitudinal studies that employ a single mode of completion, bias can be a real issue at two levels. First, respondents may choose not to respond to a particular wave of the study. This leads to **non-response bias** within each survey wave. Second, **attrition bias** can occur – that is to say, attrition from the study is not random and rather certain types of people are more likely to attrit than others. As the study progresses, this non-random attrition introduces bias. In a similar vein, even if a respondent doesn't attrit, they may choose to complete some waves of the study and not others. So, how does this matter for mode?

The use of mixed-mode surveys in a longitudinal context can be positive with regard to bias. By allowing completion in different modes, be that a sequential design or all modes up-front offer, some of the biases that may be introduced through a single mode design can be eliminated. Those who are unwilling or unable to complete in one mode can be offered an alternative that suits their needs and preferences better. As such, the achieved sample at each wave is likely to be more representative of the population of interest and therefore the data prone to fewer biases. Extending from this idea, attrition bias could also be minimised by fewer respondents dropping out of the study altogether. Offering a mixed-mode design for survey completion could encourage more participation and therefore potentially less bias.

Axinn and colleagues (2015) set out to investigate whether non-response bias was reduced in a longitudinal context by examining data from the Relationship Dynamics and Social Life (RDSL) study in the US, which adopts a mixed-mode approach. They concluded that a mixed-mode approach in this context was crucial for the success of the study in order to minimise non-response bias and attrition.

Research spotlight

Axinn, W.G., Gatny, H.H. and Wagner, J. (2015) 'Maximizing data quality using mode switching in mixed-device survey design: Nonresponse bias and models of demographic behavior'

Axinn and colleagues were interested in whether using multiple modes could lessen the impact of non-response and attrition in the context of a longitudinal study. They used data from the Relationship Dynamics and Social Life (RDSL), conducted in the US, to explore this.

The RDSL is a study that seeks to explore the links between different types of relationships and early or unplanned pregnancies. Participants are a representative sample of just over 1,000 women aged 18 to 22 who live in a single county in Michigan in the US. Study members were asked to participate in a face-to-face baseline survey and then weekly follow-ups over a period of just over three years. The weekly follow-ups were available in two modes: web and telephone. Those with the equipment and access required to complete web surveys were asked to complete their surveys in this way, although the option of telephone interviews was available to them at every wave of data collection.

Axinn and colleagues concluded that the mixed-mode design was successful in keeping respondents participating in the study and reducing bias caused by attrition. Looking at the characteristics of respondents who switched modes at one or more points in the study, they found that both demographic characteristics and characteristics related to the aims of the study (around pregnancy, etc.) differed from those participants who did not switch mode at any point. Given that those characteristics predicted who would switch mode or not, the authors were able to assert that it would be likely that if mode switching were not allowed, the resultant data would suffer from attrition bias.

(Continued)

Despite the fact that the sample were quite a specific group of people - namely, women in a narrow age range, living in a particular geographic area - the research provides compelling evidence that a mixed-mode approach in a longitudinal context is beneficial in terms of a reduction in non-response and attrition bias.

STUDY **PROFILE**

Relationship Dynamics and Social Life (RDSL)

Established: 2008.

Country: United States.

Sampling unit: individuals.

Sample size at base: 1,003 individuals.

Frequency of interviews: weekly (following a baseline survey).

Participants: 18-22-year-old women resident in Genesee County, Michigan.

Topics covered: family living arrangements, socioeconomic status, employment, media consumption, mental health, violence, personality traits, assumptions and knowledge regarding various forms of contraception, and attitudes and opinions about social life.

Methods of data collection: face-to-face at baseline, then telephone and web follow-ups.

Data availability: data are available via the study website.

More information: www.icpsr.umich.edu/web/DSDR/studies/34626

Measurement

Put simply, measurement error is the difference between the true value of something and the measured value – that is to say, in the context of a survey question, measurement error can occur when a respondent chooses a response that does not reflect the 'truth' – be that for either an attitudinal or behavioural concept. But why is measurement error a problem in a mixed-mode survey?

As we have already learned in Chapters 8 and 9, some types of questions are more prone to measurement error in certain modes. For example, questions that are perceived as sensitive to a respondent, such as asking about their use of illegal drugs, may be best administered in a mode that does not rely on an interviewer – for example, online. This is because respondents may see non-interviewer modes as more private and may not wish to disclose potentially sensitive or socially undesirable behaviours or views to an interviewer, such as in a face-to-face interview or telephone survey.

Now imagine a mixed-mode survey in which some respondents are asked face-to-face about drug use and some are asked the same thing but online. It is likely that among the face-to-face respondents, reported use of illegal drugs is much lower than the online respondents. This may not actually be the truth, but rather measurement error has been introduced because of the mode in which the respondent has chosen, or been asked, to complete the survey.

Now think about the same example in a longitudinal context. In one wave, a respondent may be offered the opportunity to complete the survey online. They do so and report using illegal drugs. However, in the next wave, a mixed-mode approach may not be employed, and instead all respondents are asked to complete the survey face-to-face. The same respondent, despite still using illegal drugs, may not feel comfortable disclosing that information to an interviewer, so they say they don't use drugs. If you look at the data over time, it appears that this respondent previously used illegal drugs but, at some point, stopped doing so. However, this may not actually be the case and could instead be measurement error introduced through the choice of modes to offer respondents at different waves of a study.

Dillman and colleagues (2009) were interested in the impact of a sequential mixed-mode design on response rates and measurement, wondering what the trade-off was between the potential for increasing response rates versus the possibility of not obtaining comparable data between different modes.

Research spotlight

Dillman, D., Phelps, G., Tortora, R., Swift, K., Kohrell, J., Berck, J. and Messer, B.L. (2009) 'Response rate and measurement differences in mixed-mode surveys using mail, telephone, interactive voice response (IVR) and the Internet'

Dillman and colleagues set out to explore whether using multiple modes in a sequential fashion would improve response rates. They were also interested in measurement differences between modes. Using an experimental design, they allocated different households to receive different modes in different orders. For households that did not respond to the first mode they were allocated to, a different mode was offered. The study focused on four different combinations of modes:

1. Mail, then telephone.
2. Telephone, then mail.
3. Interactive voice response (IVR), then telephone.
4. Web, then telephone.

(Continued)

Their first finding - perhaps unsurprisingly, given what we have learned in previous chapters - was that response rates across treatment groups for the original mode offered were very varied. The lowest was for the web survey, at 13 per cent, up to 75 per cent for the mail survey (bear in mind that this survey was conducted in the early part of the twenty-first century, so internet penetration and device ownership was not widespread, as it is now). However, for all four experimental groups, response rates were improved by offering a second mode to non-responders, providing evidence for the argument that, if possible, mixed-mode surveys can be beneficial for improving response.

However, mixed mode surveys may impact negatively on measurement. Dillman and colleagues indeed found significant differences for mean responses to some variables across modes. Looking just at respondents from the first phase of data collection in each experimental group, they found differences between those responding to the mail survey and those completing the survey on the telephone. Telephone respondents were more likely to pick the extreme positive response to some scales compared with mail respondents. This was similar for IVR respondents versus mail respondents, with the IVR respondents again more likely to pick more positive responses than the mail sample, and for web versus telephone respondents, with telephone respondents more positive. However, comparing mail responses to web responses yielded few differences.

The authors then wondered whether these effects could be explained by looking at differences between responses to the visual modes (mail and web) versus the aural modes (telephone and IVR). After controlling for demographic differences (to remove selection bias as a confounding factor), the results show that there were indeed significant differences in responses to many items between those responding using visual modes and those responding using aural modes.

In conclusion, Dillman and colleagues recognised that using a sequential mixed-mode approach could indeed lead to high response rates, but at the cost of obtaining different answers depending on which modes were used.

How do we deal with mixed-mode longitudinal designs when using data?

So, what does all of this mean for the end user of longitudinal data? As has been demonstrated, it is crucial to understand which modes have been used for each wave of a study and also whether mixed-mode designs were implemented within a study. Longitudinal datasets will usually come with technical reports, which set out the design strategy for a particular wave of data collection. The data itself will also likely come with a flag at the respondent level, which indicates the mode of completion at each wave of the study (if multiple options have been offered to respondents at a particular wave).

Further to this, studies will often very helpfully provide weights to account for potential biases in the data caused by mode choices. The weights should account for selection biases so that the achieved sample for each wave of the study is representative of the target population. This can overcome any issues with the sample and attrition. See Chapter 4 for more information on weighting data in a longitudinal context.

The next factor to consider is measurement. As a user of longitudinal data, if there are substantive variables of interest, it is a good first step to compare responses to these measures across different modes. Once demographic variables, such as gender, age, ethnicity and socioeconomic background have been taken into account, do responses to the key measures of interest look the same across modes? If the answer to this question is 'yes', then you can be very confident in using these variables in any subsequent modelling or analysis. If the answer is 'no', on the other hand, this could be problematic for analysis. It might be, in this instance, that any interesting findings from the resultant analysis could be driven by mode effects rather than 'real' effects in the population. Readers are advised to scrutinise the data from mixed-mode designs carefully before proceeding with analysis to ensure that the results they obtain are robust and reliable.

CONCLUSIONS

This chapter has discussed the implications of using mixed or multiple modes in the context of a longitudinal study. We have seen that while there can certainly be benefits of doing so, particularly in increasing response rates and reducing costs, there can also be negative consequences. These unintended consequences centre around bias and measurement, two key things to consider when using longitudinal data.

Key learning points

- No one survey mode offers clear advantages over others, and instead the choice is a trade-off. Decisions made about which mode a study uses can be taken based on the pros and cons of each method, based on the type of questions being asked - for example, are they sensitive or not? - or on the profile of respondents - for example, will most of them have access to the internet or a telephone?
- Varying survey mode within or between waves of a longitudinal study is known as a mixed-mode approach.
- The consequences of different mode choices can have an impact on the data produced by a longitudinal study in a number of different ways. This could relate to a number of areas:
    - Response rates and attrition: offering respondents the opportunity to complete a survey in different modes may result in more people completing the survey overall, due to people being offered completion options which they prefer or are more comfortable with. However, switching modes across different waves of a longitudinal study could have the opposite impact. If a respondent is used to participating in the study in one mode, suddenly being offered a different mode may increase their reluctance to participate.

(Continued)

- Bias: by allowing completion in different modes, be that a sequential design or all up-front offer, some of the biases which may be introduced through a single mode design can be eliminated. Those who are unwilling or unable to complete in one mode can be offered an alternative which suits their needs and preferences better. As such, the achieved sample at each wave of a longitudinal study is likely to be more representative of the population of interest and therefore the data prone to fewer biases.
- Measurement: mixed-mode surveys may be more problematic in terms of measurement error. Some types of questions administered in some modes are more prone to measurement error; by asking the same questions in different modes, different levels of measurement error may be introduced, making comparison of responses from participants in different modes difficult.

- It is crucial to understand which modes have been used for each wave of a study and also whether mixed-mode designs were implemented within a study. This allows the data user to understand the potential biases and errors that may have been introduced through a mixed-mode design and also potentially account for some of them - for example, through the use of weights.

Check your understanding

1. Why might longitudinal studies choose to employ a mixed-mode design?
2. What might the negative consequences be for using different modes at different waves of a longitudinal study?
3. Briefly describe the advantages of using multiple modes within a single wave of a longitudinal study.
4. Why should a user of longitudinal data be aware of measurement error when looking at data from a mixed-mode survey?

WANT TO FIND OUT MORE?

The resources below are great sources of additional information on the content covered in this section.

For guidelines on mixed-mode design:

'Mixed-mode questionnaires and survey implementation', in Dillman, D.A., Smyth, J.D. and Christian, L.M. (2014) *Internet, Phone, Mail, and Mixed-Mode Surveys. The Tailored Design Method* (4th edn). Hoboken, NJ: John Wiley & Sons.

For more on measurement effects in a mixed-mode survey context:

Cernat, A. and Sakshaug, J.W. (2021) 'Estimating the measurement effects of mixed modes in longitudinal studies: Current practice and issues', in Lynn, P. (ed.) *Advances in Longitudinal Survey Methodology*. Hoboken, NJ: Wiley.

11

ANALYSING LONGITUDINAL DATA

OVERVIEW OF CONTENT

This chapter will introduce issues to consider when preparing analysis data, under two main headings. First, the structure of longitudinal data will be discussed. Then, the chapter will present some of the analytical techniques that are unique to longitudinal data – those methods that capitalise on the nature of longitudinal nature and allow the assessment of stability, change or trajectories over time to be analysed. The chapter will not instruct the reader on how to utilise these methods in a step-by-step way, but rather will introduce the concepts and allow the reader to understand what specific methods will allow and direct them to further resources.

The chapter explores the following methods which can be used to analyse longitudinal data:

- fixed effects models;
- random effects models;
- event history analysis (survival analysis);
- sequence analysis;
- latent class growth modelling.

Learning outcomes

After you have read this chapter, you will be able to:

- understand the structure of longitudinal data and implication for subsequent analysis;
- understand how fixed and random effects models can be used with longitudinal data;
- understand how event history analysis and sequence analysis can be used with longitudinal data;
- understand how latent class growth modelling can be used with longitudinal data.

HOW TO ANALYSE LONGITUDINAL DATA

The unique nature of longitudinal data means that specific analytical techniques should be used. Part of this is due to the structure of the data in many cases and part is due to the nature of how the data has been collected – the same individuals are interviewed at different time points, so the samples at each wave are not independent of each other. However, the very nature of longitudinal data opens up some interesting and insightful analytical opportunities too.

The aim of this chapter is not to give you the specific steps needed to undertake different kinds of analysis using longitudinal data, nor is it a comprehensive set of assumptions related to each method. Rather, it gives you information about various analytical techniques to be able to understand what methods are available and help choose the most appropriate, depending on the research question and the data available.

THE STRUCTURE OF LONGITUDINAL DATA

Let's start with the most basic part of analysis – the raw data. By its nature, longitudinal data is often structured in a different way from cross-sectional data, so that it can represent responses from the same individuals at multiple points in time. The data can be in wide or long format. Wide format simply means that for each individual or sampling unit, one row of data exists. Each measurement, at each point in time, for each sampling unit, is entered into the same row in the data. Long format, on the other hand, contains multiple rows per individual. Usually this means that for each point in time, for each individual, one row exists that contains data for all measures from a single wave of data collection. As such, there will be multiple rows for each individual, each row representing a different wave of the study. Figure 11.1 illustrates an example: each sampling unit has an ID and has participated in a test at three waves of a study. The same data are presented in both wide and long format. This might sound really basic, but it's clearly crucial to understand how the data are structured before beginning any analysis.

Wide format

Unit ID	Score Wave 1	Score Wave 2	Score Wave 3
1	28	29	25
2	10	10	15
3	35	24	11

Long format

Unit ID	Wave	Score
1	1	28
1	2	29
1	3	25
2	1	10
2	2	10
2	3	15
3	1	35
3	2	24
3	3	11

Figure 11.1 Longitudinal data presented in wide and long format

The second facet of data structure that is important to understand relates to the original sampling of sampling units (whether they are households or individuals). Very often in surveys, be that longitudinal or cross-sectional, the sampling units are not chosen purely randomly across every eligible unit. There are two common manipulations of the sampling frame which are carried out (the reasons for which will be explained in the following paragraphs): 1) stratification; 2) clustering.

Let's start with stratification. Stratification means dividing the sampling frame into groups that have similar characteristics and then choosing a sample from each of those groups or strata. By choosing a sample in this way, we can improve the precision of estimates from the survey. It also means that a smaller sample may be required to represent the entire population, which in the context of a longitudinal study can save a lot of money. Additionally, if the strata are chosen based on subpopulations or subgroups of interest, we can conduct analysis of those subgroups in particular. An example of where a stratified sampling approach might be useful would be conducting a survey in the United Kingdom. The UK is made up of four separate countries – England, Wales, Scotland and Northern Ireland. England contains most of the population of the UK. If we took a simple random sample of UK residents, we would likely end up with a significant proportion of respondents in England and not very few in each of the other three countries. In turn, this would mean that we may not be able to do an analysis of the residents of Wales, Scotland or Northern Ireland separately. By creating strata based on the country of residence, we could over-sample from the three smaller countries to ensure that analysis could be conducted on the UK sample as a whole, but also separately for each country. Stratification, by its nature, means that not every individual in a population has the same chance of being selected to participate in a survey. We will cover how to deal with that analysis later in this chapter.

As well as stratification, clustering is often also used in sample selection. This is particularly true in face-to-face surveys, where an interviewer is required to physically travel to a particular location to conduct an interview. In order to ensure that the survey is conducted efficiently, some level of clustering occurs – that is to say, multiple units are chosen from the same geographic area, resulting in 'clusters' of interviews. This saves interviewers from having to travel large distances to interview people for the study, which in turn can result in a cost saving. However, this can have an impact on the resultant data. Clustering can cause homogeneity among respondents. Homogeneity simply means 'being the same'. In the context of a survey, having multiple respondents who are at some level the same means that the entire sample may not accurately reflect the population of interest. Why might sample clustering cause homogeneity? It may be that people who live in the same geographic area are more likely to share certain characteristics. For example, they may be more likely to be wealthy (as they can afford to purchase a home in an area where house prices are relatively high compared to other areas) or they may be more likely to come from a particular ethnic background (we know that in most countries the ethnic diversity of the population does not extend to all geographic areas). By unintentionally over-sampling particular groups through the use of a clustered sample design, some groups will be undersampled and therefore under-represented in the data. As with stratification, this needs to be accounted for in analysis of the data, which will be discussed later.

Third, the choice of sampling units themselves can add another layer of complexity to the data. If the individual is the sampling unit, this tends to be less complex; each individual is independent of one another (barring the issue with clustering, discussed above). If the household has been sampled as the unit and then multiple individuals within that household are interviewed, the structure of the data becomes a little different giving it a hierarchical structure. Now you have individuals nested within households. Given that individuals within households may share certain characteristics, this may need to be accounted for in analysis. These characteristics could relate to things like income, as discussed above. Individuals living in the same household may have access to the same level of disposable income as one another, making them reasonably homogeneous. There could also be similarities in behaviours and also attitudes. As such, people within a household are likely to be more homogeneous than people living in different households. Again, this is something that should be considered before conducting analysis. Additionally, having a nested structure may also influence the type of methods that can be used to conduct analysis.

The next section explains how to account for the structure of longitudinal data when deciding how to analyse it. The following section then covers some common methods used for analysis.

Accounting for the structure of longitudinal data

The section above demonstrated that the structure of longitudinal data, particularly related to the sample design, can have an impact on who is in the sample and how those individuals are related. As such, the resultant analysis from this data is likely to be biased, unless we do something to account for the original structure and sampling. So how can we account for this?

The most common way to account for the sample design of a longitudinal study is weighting. Most longitudinal studies use a sampling method where the chances of selection for each individual are known (see Chapter 3 for more on sampling). With a stratified or clustered sample, the probability of selection for each individual is calculable – it is not equal, but it is known. As such, weights can be calculated to account for the sample design. These are usually called 'design weights' (see Chapter 4 for more information on weighting), and many longitudinal studies will calculate and release these weights alongside the data. It is really important that researchers use these weights in any analysis of the data to ensure that the data really reflects the population it is intended to reflect.

In terms of data that are in a nested structure – most commonly, individuals within sampled households – the answer to dealing with this structure is often also through weighting. Again, these weights tend to be supplied alongside the data.

METHODS FOR ANALYSING LONGITUDINAL DATA

This section will give an overview of some of the methods that are commonly used to analyse longitudinal data, explaining when it is appropriate to use and what it can tell you.

It is important to choose a method that is specifically designed to be used for longitudinal data due to the nature of longitudinal data. Given that the same individual is asked the same question at multiple points in time, the data for that measure within each individual is correlated. Methods not designed for longitudinal data may not account for that correlation, causing problems with outputs.

Fixed effects models

Fixed effects models are a type of exploratory model. Exploratory models are fairly self-explanatory: an approach to data in which we explore what the data shows us, rather than necessarily having fixed hypotheses when we start analysis. The research questions we can answer using fixed effects models amount to those that ask, 'Does a change in one variable cause a change in an outcome of interest?'.

Fixed effects models can be applied to longitudinal data because they control for all confounds that are time-invariant – those things that do not change over time – and that includes those confounding factors that are both observed (something we have measured) and unobserved (something we haven't measured). The model does this by using only the changes in exposure to particular circumstances or events occurring within individuals to estimate the outcome. This, however, is also the major assumption of the model: that the time-invariant things really are time-invariant.

In the context of a longitudinal study, the fixed effects can be unobservable things that are intrinsic to each individual and are presumed to be related to outcomes of interest, but do not change over time.

Fixed effects models

What kinds of research questions will these models help me to answer?

- Questions that are exploratory in nature.
- Questions that are trying to figure out whether change in one variable causes a change in an outcome of interest.

When can I use these models?

- When an explanatory variable has a fixed or constant relationship with the response variable across over time.

However, there are some variables that we are interested in modelling that are not necessarily fixed – in other words, they change over time. These could be things like employment status or welfare receipt. These can be incorporated into a fixed effects model by including dummy variables. Dummy variables are those where the variable takes the value of 0 or 1, depending on the absence or presence of something. In a longitudinal context, dummy variables could be used for time-varying factors at each wave of data collection. Alternatively, a random effects model may be more appropriate.

Random effects models

Random effects models (also referred to as 'generalised linear mixed models') are a special type of fixed effects model. Instead of some model parameters being fixed over time, as in the fixed effects model, they are allowed instead to be random to some extent. The underlying assumption is that the measurements from each individual in the dataset share a set of random effects that are not observed or measured, allowing for model parameters to have a random element. A further assumption is that this individual unobserved heterogeneity (or, in other words, differences between people that are not measured) is not correlated with any of the independent variables in the model.

There are many different ways to set up a random effects model, depending on the data and outcomes of interest. Tzavidis and colleagues (2016), for example, used an approach that was new at the time, which they called 'M-quantile random-effects regression', to analyse strengths and difficulties data from the Millennium Cohort Study in the UK.

Research spotlight

Tzavidis, N., Salvati, N., Schmid, T., Flouri, E. and Midouhas, E. (2016) 'Longitudinal analysis of the strengths and difficulties questionnaire scores of the Millennium Cohort Study children in England using M-quantile random-effects regression'

The Millennium Cohort Study (MCS), as we have seen in previous chapters, is a longitudinal study of children born at the turn of the century in the UK. In many waves of the study, the strengths and difficulties questionnaire (SDQ) has been used, which assesses emotional and behavioural symptoms and problems in children and young people. Tzavidis and colleagues set out to use the SDQ responses across three waves of MCS to look at the effect that various risk factors related to a child's family and neighbourhood had on behavioural and emotional problems.

Using their novel M-quantile random-effects regression approach, they were able to determine a number of things with regard to SDQ scores. They found that male children tended to have higher scores than female children (with a higher score indicating the presence of more emotional and behavioural problems). Additionally, a range of other variables were related to higher SDQ scores, including socioeconomic disadvantage and deprivation at the neighbourhood level, as well as maternal depression and a lower level of maternal education.

What was especially interesting about this specific random-effects approach was that it seemed to be a particularly efficient way to model data that are clustered.

Random effects models

What kinds of research questions will these models help me to answer?

- Questions that are exploratory in nature.
- Questions that are trying to figure out whether change in one variable causes a change in an outcome of interest.

When can I use these models?

- When the explanatory variable does not have a fixed or constant relationship with the response variable over time.

Event history analysis (survival analysis)

Moving on from fixed-effects models, event history analysis, also known as survival analysis, refers to a set of analytical techniques that are used to understand or predict occurrences of an event. This is a different approach to analysing longitudinal data. Event history analysis is only possible when you have longitudinal data because the technique requires knowledge about past events to predict future ones. In the social sciences, these 'events' can be related to a broad range of things – for example, fertility, death, job status change, and so on.

Of particular interest to researchers conducting event history is looking at the factors that predict the timing of a particular event occurring. A good example is work carried out by Berrington and Diamond (2000) who used event history analysis to look at the age of first partnership among a cohort of people born in 1958 in Great Britain.

Research spotlight

Berrington, A. and Diamond, I. (2000) 'Marriage or cohabitation: A competing risks analysis of first-partnership formation among the 1958 British birth cohort'

Berrington and Diamond were interested in exploring what predicted the age of first partnership among a cohort of individuals born in 1958. They used data from the National Child Development Study (NCDS), which is a longitudinal study of individuals born in Great Britain in 1958. NCDS conducted interviews with cohort members at multiple points in time, collecting rich information on education, health, social background and many other domains. This enabled the implementation of an event history analysis to establish factors that could predict the age at which individuals entered into their first partnership - the 'event'.

The authors were able to identify a number of factors that affected when the first partnership for an individual was likely to occur, as well as the type of that partnership - that is to say, whether that partnership was marriage or cohabitation. One of the key factors identified was education. They established that both men and women who obtained a degree or equivalent were more likely to delay their first partnership formation until their late 20s, and were also more likely to opt to cohabit rather than marry in the first instance. Additionally, those who reported being less religious were more likely to cohabit rather than marry in their first partnership, and those whose parents have separated are more likely to initially cohabit rather than marry.

The findings in the paper are far more extensive than those included here, but the examples highlighted demonstrate how the richness of longitudinal data can be used to predict events and outcomes using event history analysis.

As the research by Berrington and Diamond demonstrates, the richness of longitudinal data, captured across the life-course, lends itself perfectly to event history analysis when a researcher is interested in predicting the occurrence of an event.

A key concept that researchers should be aware of when undertaking survival analysis is censoring. This is when complete data is not available for all people – cases where we don't have information about the timing of the event of interest for all the people we are interested in. An example of this in a longitudinal context, using the Berrington and Diamond research above, would be where people dropped out of the NCDS study before they entered their first partnership. For many study participants, there would be information about when they entered their first partnership, but some may have dropped out of the study before the event occurred. This is known as 'right censoring'. 'Left censoring', on the other hand, is where an event has occurred during the study period, but we aren't entirely sure when it occurred. Using the partnership example, an individual might report not having a partner in one interview. However, in their follow-up interview some years later, they report having a partner, but no information is collected on when this occurred. If we are interested in age of first partnership, we know that the event has occurred, but we don't know specifically at what age.

If it is not handled correctly, censoring can bias results from a survival analysis. Censoring can either be handled in the same way that you would handle missing data (as it can be seen as a special form of missing data), such as by using complete case analysis or imputation (see Chapter 4 for more information) or using more nuanced methods. See Turkson et al. (2021), who conducted a systematic review of the literature on how censoring has been handled by researchers.

Survival analysis

What kinds of research questions will these models help me to answer?

- Questions that want to explore the time to an event of interest occurring.

When can I use these models?

- When I want to explore what predicts an event occurring at a particular time.

STUDY **PROFILE**

National Child Development Study (NCDS)

Established: 1958.

Country: Great Britain.

Sampling unit: individuals.

Sample size at base: 17,415.

Frequency of interviews: irregularly - surveys at birth, age 7, 11, 16, 23, 33, 42, 46, 50, 55, 62.

(Continued)

Participants: everybody born in a particular week in England, Wales and Scotland in 1958.

Topics covered: physical and educational development, economic circumstances, employment, family life, health behaviour, well-being, social participation and attitudes.

Methods of data collection: face-to-face interviews, paper self-completion questionnaires, telephone, web.

Innovative features: bio-measure collection, data linkage.

Data availability: data are available to the research community via the UK Data Service.

More information: https://cls.ucl.ac.uk/cls-studies/1958-national-child-development-study/

Sequence analysis

Sequence analysis is an extension of event history analysis. Instead of looking at single events in isolation and predicting the occurrence of those events, sequence analysis takes sequences of events at an individual level to look at individual trajectories. As with event history analysis, sequence analysis is actually a term for multiple different methods that all aim to achieve the same outcome.

By taking the sequence approach, researchers can establish what a 'typical' life-course looks like, as well as alternative trajectories. In addition, these trajectories, or sequences, can then be compared across different groups to look at differences or similarities between groups. The groups could be different generations or different geographical areas, for example.

Research spotlight

Schoon, I., Ross, A. and Martin, P. (2009) 'Sequences, patterns, and variations in the assumption of work and family-related roles: Evidence from two British birth cohorts'

Schoon and colleagues set out to explore the patterns of transitions into adulthood, and specifically how they were changing across generations. Using data from the National Child Development Study (NCDS) and the 1970 British Cohort Study (BCS70), they were able to use sequence analysis to look at patterns in transitions to adulthood among two cohorts of individuals born in Great Britain in two different years - 1958 and 1970.

In this case, transitions were defined as events (in the same way as event history analysis), which indicated a change in some domain of life. Rather than using a single event, the authors looked at multiple events and the order in which they occurred within individuals. Such events could be leaving full-time education, entering further education, starting a full-time job, becoming unemployed, and so on.

Sequence analysis in this case produced 17 typologies, or trajectories, observed across the two datasets - that is to say, there were 17 distinct paths taken by the individuals studied in transitioning from adolescence into adulthood. However, when the researchers looked at the two datasets separately - the one containing individuals born in 1958 and the one containing individuals born in 1970 - they realised that there was more diversity in trajectories in the group born in 1970 than those born in 1958. Therefore, they came to the conclusion that life-course diversification had occurred over time - that is to say, people born later were taking more diverse paths into adulthood than the generation born before them. The paper also contains a multitude of additional aspects, including looking at trajectories by gender, as well as social background.

This research demonstrates the importance of rich longitudinal data and how sequence analysis can be used to explore it in great depth.

The research by Schoon and colleagues shows how sequence analysis is a good analytical choice for researchers interested in predicting trajectories over the life-course, something only possible with longitudinal data.

Sequence analysis

What kinds of research questions will these models help me to answer?

- Questions that want to explore the time to an event of interest occurring.

When can I use these models?

- When I want to explore what predicts an event occurring at a particular time for different people.

Latent class growth modelling

As with previous analytical techniques discussed in this chapter, latent growth modelling is an approach to modelling, rather than a single method. It is an approach that is only possible when using longitudinal data. As the name suggests, these analytical techniques look at growth trajectories, or how different people end up on different paths. A simple example to illustrate growth trajectories could be weight. Using data taken at multiple time points in a longitudinal study of children, researchers are often interested in how weight increases as the child ages and the factors that contribute to different trajectories of weight gain. Latent growth modelling could be used to assess this. However, the concept being measured doesn't have to involve explicit physical growth and the modelling technique can be applied to a wide array of measures a researcher could be interested in, such as other domains of child development, personality or various biomarkers.

The second key component of the name is 'latent class'. These models are particularly useful for looking at populations that appear to be heterogeneous (in other words, where there exists a mixture of completely different types of people or things) and identifying subgroups within the population that are homogeneous (people or things which are more similar, sharing key characteristics). These identified subgroups become latent classes. This means that rather than assuming the same growth trajectory for an entire population, the technique allows different growth patterns to be identified from each homogeneous subgroup or latent class.

A good example of this method in action is research by Baek and Choi (2021) who used a latent class growth model to examine alcohol use behaviours, and changes in that behaviour, among a sample of Korean adults.

Research spotlight

Baek, A. and Choi, E.H. (2021) 'A longitudinal analysis of alcohol use behavior among Korean adults and related factors: A latent class growth model'

Baek and Choi were interested in understanding the trajectories of alcohol use behaviours in adults through identifying different latent classes of behaviour and associated trajectories, and exploring the different factors associated with different trajectories. Ultimately, analysis such as this could allow policy-makers to better target and implement programmes to improve alcohol use behaviour.

The researchers used eleven waves of data from the Korea Welfare Panel Study (KoWePS), a longitudinal study of Korean households, looking at responses from adults of legal drinking age in Korea. Using responses to a self-reported scale about alcohol use, alongside a range of variables measuring demographics, mental health status and life satisfaction, Baek and Choi were able to assess latent classes and associated trajectories of alcohol use behaviour.

They first identified four latent classes of alcohol use behaviour within the longitudinal dataset: 'moderate- to low-risk class', 'low- to moderate-risk class', 'stable moderate-risk class' and 'stable low-risk class'. The first two classes indicate changes in trajectories - from moderate risk down to low risk over time, low risk up to moderate risk over time, and two classes where risk is stable over the course of the analytical period.

The researchers found that as individuals became older, the incidence of high-risk alcohol use behaviour decreased. Additionally, individuals aged 19-49 years had a higher likelihood of belonging to the 'low- to moderate-risk class' or 'stable moderate-risk class' than 'moderate- to low-risk class', compared with those aged 50-60. They also found that male participants were more likely to engage in high-risk alcohol use behaviours than women, with women more likely to be in the 'stable low-risk class'. Individuals who were unemployed were also most likely to appear in the 'stable low-risk class'. However, those who were part of single-person families - for example, people who were divorced or widowed - were more likely to belong to higher risk classes. In terms of satisfaction with family relationships, satisfaction was the highest in the 'low- to moderate-risk class', but it decreased over time to be the lowest by the final wave included in the analysis. The opposite pattern was seen where satisfaction with family relationships was lowest in the 'moderate- to low-risk class', but increased over time. Baek and Choi's paper contains far more findings than the few briefly outlined here.

The authors are able to conclude their analysis with a recommendation with real-world impact around policy implementation. They suggest that in Korea, there is a need for drinking prevention education and intervention, as well as culture change in specific areas and among specific groups of people.

Baek and Choi's findings illustrate the power of longitudinal data and subsequent latent growth modelling for understanding complex issues at play in the world today.

STUDY **PROFILE**

Korea Welfare Panel Study (KoWePS)

Established: 1958.

Country: Korea.

Sampling unit: households.

Sample size at base: 7,000 households.

Frequency of interviews: annual.

Participants: households in Korean identified via the 2C05 census, excluding islands and special facilities.

Topics covered: economic circumstances, employment, education, medical care, living conditions, use of welfare services, life satisfaction, family relationships.

Methods of data collection: face-to-face interviews, self-completion questionnaires.

Data availability: data are available to the research community via the UK Data Service.

More information: https://cls.ucl.ac.uk/cls-studies/1958-national-child-development-study/

Latent class growth modelling

What kinds of research questions will these models help me to answer?

- Questions that want to explore different trajectories for different groups of people.

When can I use these models?

- When there are truly differences in trajectories between different groups within the population of interest.

CONCLUSIONS

This chapter has given an overview of two aspects to consider when analysing longitudinal data. The first is the structure of the data, related both to how it was collected, but also how the original sample was drawn and the influence that has on the structure. The second are some analytical methods that can be used on longitudinal data.

A whole wealth of information is available on the analytical methods appropriate for longitudinal data, and it is an area that is evolving over time, with new or adapted methods constantly being introduced. This book does not have the space to be able to do justice to this area, and as such has given a flavour rather than a comprehensive account. Readers are recommended to consult publications whose aim is specifically to teach the detail of longitudinal analysis if they wish to conduct their own analysis of longitudinal data.

Key learning points

- The unique nature of longitudinal data means that specific analytical techniques should be used be used. Part of this is due to the structure of the data in many cases and part is due to the nature of how the data has been collected.
- Longitudinal data is often structured in a different way from cross-sectional data to represent responses from the same individuals at multiple points in time. The data can be in wide or long format.
    - Wide format means that for each individual, or sampling unit, one row of data exists.
    - Long format contains multiple rows per individual.
- It is important to understand how the original sampling was conducted prior to analysis. Two common manipulations of the sampling frame are carried out:

    - Stratification: dividing the sampling frame into groups that have similar characteristics and then choosing a sample from each of those groups or strata.
    - Clustering: where multiple units are chosen from the same geographic area, resulting in 'clusters' of interviews.
- Third, the choice of sampling units themselves can add another layer of complexity to the data. For example, if the household has been sampled as the unit and then multiple individuals within that household are interviewed, the structure of the data becomes a little different, giving it a hierarchical structure. Now you have individuals nested within households.
- The most common way to account for sample design decisions is weighting.
- A multitude of analytical techniques are unique to longitudinal data to allow researchers to understand change, stability and trajectories over time. Some of the most common ones are:
    - Fixed effects models: a type of exploratory model. The research questions we can answer using fixed effects models amount to those that ask, 'Does a change in one variable cause a change in an outcome of interest?'. Fixed effects models can be applied to longitudinal data because they control for all confounds that are time-invariant.
    - Random effects models: a special type of fixed effects model. Instead of some model parameters being fixed over time, as in the fixed effects model, they are allowed instead to be random to some extent.
    - Event history analysis (survival analysis): a set of analytical techniques that are used to understand or predict occurrences of an event.
    - Sequence analysis: an extension of event history analysis. Instead of looking at single events in isolation and predicting the occurrence of those events, sequence analysis takes sequences of events at an individual level to look at individual trajectories.
    - Latent class growth modelling. These analytical techniques look at growth trajectories for multiple homogeneous subsections of a population.

Check your understanding

1. What is the difference between wide format and long format data?
2. What are the aspects of sample design that need to be taken into account prior to analysis?
3. List some research questions that could be answered using fixed or random effects models.
4. What does event history analysis allow a researcher to understand?
5. List some research questions that could be answered using latent class growth modelling techniques.

WANT TO FIND OUT MORE?

The resources below are great sources of additional information on the content discussed in this section.

Fitzmaurice, G., Davidian, M., Verbeke, G. and Molenberghs, G. (eds) (2008) *Longitudinal Data Analysis*. Boca Raton, FL: CRC Press.

Gayle, V. and Lambert, P. (2020) *Quantitative Longitudinal Data Analysis*. London: Bloomsbury Publishing.

Wang, Y., Fu, L. and Paul, S. (2022) *Analysis of Longitudinal Data with Examples*. Boca Raton, FL: CRC Press.

12

TALKING ABOUT LONGITUDINAL DATA

OVERVIEW OF CONTENT

This chapter will bring together everything you have learned in the previous chapters and frame it in the context of writing about longitudinal data. We will look at the key pieces of information that should be reported when writing about longitudinal data analysis, and the importance of doing so in an open and transparent way.

Additionally, the chapter will explore why we may choose to use longitudinal data to answer a research question despite any limitations with the dataset and explain how to defend that choice.

Learning outcomes

After you have read this chapter, you will be able to:

- list the key pieces of information you should include when you are writing or talking about longitudinal data analysis;
- understand why it's important to give readers as much information as possible about how the analysis of longitudinal datasets has been conducted;
- be able to defend your choice of using a particular longitudinal dataset to answer a research question.

HOW TO DISCUSS AND WRITE ABOUT LONGITUDINAL DATA

Longitudinal data is unique. It's that uniqueness which makes it a popular choice for researchers interested in a wide array of subjects and research questions.

So far, this book has discussed a multitude of issues related to longitudinal data, be that related to sampling, data-collection mode, question types, attrition or panel conditioning. Each of these are important factors when thinking about both using longitudinal data, but also when writing or speaking about it.

This chapter will look at how longitudinal data should be reported on, taking into account the things that are unique to longitudinal data that have been covered in previous chapters.

REPORTING ON LONGITUDINAL DATA: KEY INFORMATION

When reporting on any research, longitudinal or otherwise, researchers should think carefully about the information they need to include to ensure that readers have a full and transparent understanding of the research. At the most fundamental level, the work should make absolutely clear what the topic of interest is and the research questions stemming from that. Beyond these, there are three key areas that should be explicitly discussed in order to ensure transparency – study design, missing data and attrition, and analytical techniques – which are considered in the sections below.

Study design

Study basics

Starting with the most basic of information, it is crucial to report which study you have used data from. However, beyond this, there are other key pieces of information about a study that are essential to report to report. First, which country or countries do the data come from? This allows the reader to understand in which contexts your results may be applicable. Additionally, some longitudinal studies are based in a single country, whereas others, such as Young Lives, cover multiple countries. It is important for people looking at your research to understand whether you have used just one country in your analysis, whether data from multiple countries have been pooled together, or whether you have conducted multiple analyses on different pools of data independently.

Delving a little deeper into this, it is important to be clear what the target population for the study that you are talking about is. It could be that the study aims to represent the entire adult population of a country, a cohort of people born in a particular year or under particular circumstances, or something else entirely. You should first be aware of what the dataset is intended to be representative of, and also make that clear in any outputs you produce.

STUDY **PROFILE**

Young Lives

Established: 2001.

Country: Ethiopia, India, Peru and Vietnam.

Sampling unit: individuals.

Sample size at base: c. 12,000.

Frequency of interviews: irregular (2002, 2006/7, 2009/10, 2013/14, 2016/17, plus additional COVID-related data collection in 2020)

Participants: Cohort 1: children aged between 6 and 18 months in 2002. Cohort 2: children aged between 7 and 8 years in 2002.

Topics covered: family life, nutrition, well-being, cognitive and physical development, health behaviours, education.

Methods of data collection: face-to-face interviews, telephone surveys.

Innovative features: longitudinal qualitative research with subsets of the sample, time-use data, cognitive assessments, school survey.

Data availability: data are available to the research community via the UK Data Service.

More information: www.younglives.org.uk/

Sampling information

As we have already seen, the sampling unit – that is, the single items that make up the population of interest – can vary between studies. Sampling units can be individuals, households or businesses, for example. These are the entities that are followed over time. It is important to make clear what the original sampling unit was for the study you are talking about and how it has been used in your research.

In relation to sampling, it can also be helpful to the reader to understand the sampling frame used to select study participants. Related to an earlier point, this allows an assessment of whether the target population is indeed represented by the sample of respondents selected. Extending this idea, providing information on the approach to sample selection will also allow an assessment of the robustness of the resultant sample. Discussion of any stratification or clustering, for example, will help readers to understand the potential make-up of the sample.

Time periods

Another key element to report on is which years or time periods the data you are talking about cover – have you used data from every available wave of a longitudinal study or have you restricted your analysis to a subset of available data? Understanding the time frame covered by the data allows readers of your work to again assess the applicability of results to different contexts.

Mode(s) of data collection

As previous chapters have shown us, the mode in which data are collected can have an impact on the responses received. It is important to be explicit about the mode in which the data you're reporting on has been collected. This could be a single mode for all time points of a study, or it could be different modes for different waves of data collection. You should be explicit about which mode or modes are used at each time point.

Beyond this, it might be that if you're looking at a dataset with multiple modes of data collection, you have done some work to assess comparability between modes. It would be useful to share the findings of this analysis with the reader of any outputs you have produced.

Analysis

Reporting response rates

When writing up the results of a piece of research, it is best practice to report on the response rate for the dataset you have used for analysis. This is true of most journals, but also may be a requirement for an internal report, dissertation or any other publication method. In a cross-sectional context, reporting on response rates is usually relatively straightforward as the eligible sample is usually known, along with the number of people who actually participated. In a longitudinal context, reporting response rates can become a little trickier. For example, is the base size for calculating response rates the eligible sample for a particular wave or is it the original eligible sample? It may also be necessary to report on multiple response rates – for example, response rates for each wave of data used.

Some journals, research bodies and institutions provide guidance on how they expect authors to calculate response rates. For example, the American Association for Public Opinion Research (AAPOR) have written guidance on how to calculate various types of outcomes, such as response rates, recruitment rates and refusal rates (AAPOR, 2022). Many journals that report on survey methods topics require researchers to adhere to the AAPOR guidelines and reporting definitions. The AAPOR guidance contains information on how to calculate and report these rates for longitudinal or panel data.

Analytical methods used

It is crucial to be clear in any analytical output produced, regardless of whether that analysis is based on cross-sectional or longitudinal data, which analytical methods have been chosen and why. In order for reviewers and readers to be able to assess whether the method is appropriate for the research question and the dataset, authors must provide detail on which method has been chosen. It is usually appropriate to also justify the choice of methods – why is the method or combination of methods used appropriate to answer the research question? The answer to this should also focus on the data itself, as well as the research question at hand. When writing about research based on longitudinal datasets, it is wise to justify the choice of a particular longitudinal analytical technique.

Missing data and attrition attenuation strategies

Chapter 4 covered the topic of missing data and attrition. Missing data is where data is missing in its entirety for individual respondents, or within responses from an individual where there is data missing on individual variables. Attrition is a form of missing data specific to longitudinal studies where participants of a study drop out or, as it is also known, 'attrit'– they no longer take part in the study. Missing data and attrition can have an impact on results if they are not accounted for in analysis. When reporting on longitudinal analysis, it is important to be clear on how missing data and/or attrition have been handled.

Weighting

Chapter 4 looked at weighting in the context of missing data and Chapter 11 covered the same topic in the context of analytical methods for longitudinal data. When writing about research based on longitudinal datasets, it is important to provide clarity on exactly which weights were applied to the data and why. This allows readers to assess how appropriate the dataset you are using is to answer your research questions and can provide reassurance on the robustness and accuracy of the results presented.

REPORTING ON LONGITUDINAL DATA: CONCLUSIONS

As has become evident through the course of this chapter, there is a lot of information that should be reported on when a researcher chooses to use longitudinal data to answer their research questions. From information on the study design, collected data and analytical methods, there is a huge array of detail that needs to be presented. Figure 12.1 summarises this.

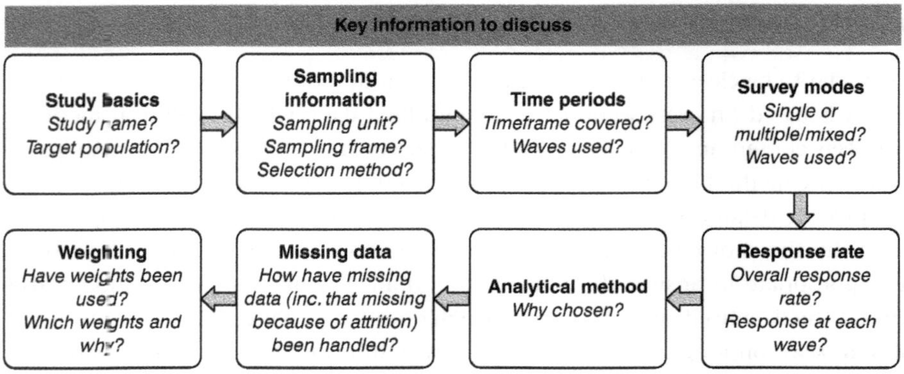

Figure 12.1 A summary of key information to include when talking about longitudinal data analysis

Why is this so important? The reasons are twofold. First, by giving readers as much information as possible about how the analysis has been conducted, they are able to draw their own conclusions about the robustness of the analytical techniques and choices, and ultimately the validity of the results. Second, by giving readers all the parameters used in a particular analysis, the research becomes replicable – that is to say, other researchers can repeat the analysis using the same techniques and choices. This is particularly important in two ways: 1) It allows researchers to test the robustness of the conclusions on a different data set; 2) It permits the replication of research on a different population to see if the conclusions still hold under different circumstances and in different contexts.

However, not all longitudinal research is currently reported on with equal robustness. Tooth and colleagues (2005) undertook some research to assess how rigorously journal articles that used longitudinal research in their analysis reported on various facets of the data and analysis. The type of research they focused on was that published in health, medicine and epidemiology journals – while that might not seem directly applicable to all readers here, the research is valuable to scholars working in fields other than these. While the research is interesting in and of itself, readers may be particularly interested in a checklist they created in order to assess the rigour of reporting longitudinal analysis.

Research spotlight

Tooth, L., Ware, R., Bain, C., Purdie, D.M. and Dobson, A. (2005) 'Quality of reporting of observational longitudinal research'

Tooth and colleagues begin their paper with an observation that there are no agreed or mandatory reporting requirements when talking about research that has been conducted using longitudinal data. In order to assess the impact of this in published journal articles, they developed a checklist of pieces of information that would be desirable to be included in published articles. The information in the checklist were the pieces of information that would allow a reader to identify key threats to both internal and external validity of a study, thus allowing an assessment of robustness.

The checklist itself contained 33 items, covering two different aspects of information provision. The first related to things about a study that could have an influence on actual results - in other words, anything that might affect estimates produced from the data. The second was wider, more descriptive aspects of a study.

The 33 criteria against which studies were evaluated can be found in the original article, which includes full definitions of each. Below is a summary.

1. Study objectives stated.
2. Target population defined.
3. Sampling frame defined.
4. Study population defined.
5. Study location/venues listed.
6. Study dates listed.
7. Eligibility criteria stated.
8. Selection/recruitment issues stated.
9. Number of participants justified.
10. Number of eligible and ireligible participants stated.
11. Eligibility criteria stated.
12. Consent rates stated.
13. Reasons for refusal stated.
14. Assessment of those who consented vs. those who did not.
15. Number of participants at the beginning of the study stated.
16. Data collection methods stated.
17. Reliability of measurement methods discussed.
18. Validity of measurement methods discussed.
19. Confounders discussed.
20. Number of participants at each wave stated.
21. Reasons for attrition stated.
22. Missing data within each wave discussed.
23. Analysis methods used.
24. Longitudinal analysis methods used.
25. Absolute effect sizes reported.
26. Relative effect sizes reported.
27. Attrition accounted for in analysis.
28. Confounders accounted for in analysis.
29. Missing data accounted for in analysis.
30. Impact of biases assessed qualitatively.
31. Impact of biases assessed quantitatively.

(Continued)

32. Results related from sample back to target population.
33. Further discussion of generalisability.

The first step for Tooth and colleagues was to code up a sample of journal articles against the checklist to see the level of inclusion of the key information in each. They found that on average, in the journal articles they coded, 17 of the 33 criteria were mentioned - that is to say, each article on average only reported on about half of the information deemed useful. Additionally, those criteria related to the study design were more likely to be reported on than those related to validity.

The authors ultimately recommended that authors should consider using their checklist when writing about longitudinal research.

While the checklist created by Tooth and colleagues may not be applicable to every longitudinal analysis you write about, it provides a neat reminder of the types of issues that may be important to discuss when talking about longitudinal data.

DEFENDING THE LIMITATIONS OF A DATASET

Everything that has been discussed in this book so far points towards the fact that longitudinal data can be extremely complex but incredibly useful for answering many research questions that would otherwise remain unanswered. However, as you will have learned, longitudinal data (and they ways you choose to use it), can also have its limitations. These include, but are not limited to:

- appropriate longitudinal data not being collected in the geographic area of interest or on the population of interest;
- missing data and attrition leading to datasets that are not complete;
- panel conditioning possibly being present in the data;
- multiple modes being used either at a single time point in data collection or across different waves.

This is not insurmountable and should not necessarily be a reason not to choose to conduct analysis using longitudinal data; after all, it is only possible to answer some research questions using longitudinal data, and sometimes some evidence is better than none at all.

However, the issues, or potential issues, which you come across with the data you are using should always be discussed in any write-up or discussion of the research. Being transparent about potential problems allows readers to make their own judgement on the robustness of analysis. Against these issues, always justify why you have decided to continue to use the dataset anyway, despite the possible problems with it.

This may be because there are no alternative datasets and the one you have is the best one available for exploring the questions you are interested in, or because there are things that you have been able to do with the data (through case selection or analytical techniques) which overcome the shortfalls of the data.

An open and transparent conversation about the shortfalls, solutions and resultant conclusions that you are able to draw from the data is so important.

CONCLUSIONS

This chapter has brought together everything explored in previous chapters, framed in the context of actually using longitudinal datasets in real-life research. Despite the complexities and sometimes downfalls of longitudinal data, you will know by now that its uniqueness is key to its importance. Without longitudinal data, there are some things that we simply wouldn't understand.

However, as with any reporting, openness and transparency is key. In order for readers to be able to understand how analysis was conducted, the robustness of the analysis and the ability of the data to answer the research questions at hand, they need to be given a lot of key pieces of information about the dataset itself. This includes information about the study design, the data collected and the analytical methods used. While a dataset may not be absolutely perfect, these issues are often not insurmountable and instead require careful thought about first how to use the data and, just as importantly, how to write about it. Hopefully, this book has armed you with the information you need in order to be able to use longitudinal data effectively to answer research questions on a myriad of topics.

Happy writing!

Key learning points

- There are a number of factors that are important to report when writing or speaking about longitudinal data.
  - Which country or countries do the data come from?
  - What is the target population of the study?
  - What is the sampling unit in the study?
  - Over what time periods were data collected or included in your analysis?
  - Which modes of data collection were used at each time point in your dataset?
  - How do missing data and attrition affect your dataset and how have they been handled in the analysis?
  - Which analytical methods have been used?
  - Have weights been used on the data and, if so, what do they account for?
- All the above issues should be reported on, as well as the impact these things have on your analysis and the decisions taken around analytical techniques.

(Continued)

- By giving readers as much information as possible about how the analysis has been conducted, they are able to draw their own conclusions about the robustness of the analytical techniques and choices, and ultimately the validity of the results.
- By giving readers all the parameters used in a particular analysis, the research becomes replicable - that is to say, other researchers can repeat the analysis using the same techniques and choices.
- The issues that you come across with the longitudinal data you're using should always be discussed in any write-up or discussion of the research.
- Always justify why you have decided to use a particular dataset.

Check your understanding

1. List the main information you should give readers about analysis conducted using longitudinal data.
2. What are two reasons for giving as much information to readers about the datasets and analytical methods you have used?
3. Why might you use an imperfect dataset to answer a research question?

Glossary

*Glossary terms in the text are **emboldened** on the first mention.*

Acquiescence bias the tendency of some respondents to agree with statements or provide responses that are positive (rather than negative). Acquiescence bias can introduce measurement error into data.

Age effects effects that are related to the biological age of an individual. Age effects are in contrast to period effects and cohort effects.

Attrition where participants of a longitudinal study drop out, or 'attrit'. There can be many reasons for attrition, including refusal, loss to follow-up, or serious illness or death. Attrition can be considered one of the major methodological problems in longitudinal studies. It can result in the sample not representing the population as a whole.

Attrition bias a type of bias introduced when attrition in a longitudinal study occurs. Attrition may not be random, as certain types of people are more likely to attrit than others. This can result in the sample not representing the population as a whole.

Balanced panel in a longitudinal dataset, all measurements are available for all sampling units for all waves. This is in contrast to an unbalanced panel.

Bias bias in statistics is where the data collected about a particular population doesn't accurately represent that population due to a systematic error in the data.

Boost samples where additional participants are added to a study, usually after it has started, with the aim of increasing the numbers of particular groups of people in the study. This makes analysis on specific subgroups of the sample possible.

Break-off in the context of a survey, a break-off is where respondents get part-way through a survey or questionnaire and then stop, failing to complete it in its entirety.

Causation where changes in one variable cause changes in a different variable and, as such, we can say that there is a cause-and-effect relationship between them. This is in contrast to correlation.

Clustered sample a type of probability sample. A clustered sample is where the population of interest is divided into different groups, called clusters, and then a sample of those groups is drawn. From within these clusters, a selection of sampling units are then chosen. A clustered sample is often used when the population of interest is distributed over large geographic areas. Choosing clusters of sample members can make the research more efficient and cost-effective.

Cohort effects effects that are unique to a specific group of people based on a common factor between them and common experiences or occurrences across time. Cohort effects are in contrast to age effects and period effects.

Cohort studies a type of longitudinal study that follows a group of people over time who all share a particular characteristic. Most commonly, these are birth cohorts, where individuals were all born in the same year, but they could also be a group of people who graduated from high school or university in the same year or worked for a particular company at a certain time, for example.

Construct theoretical things we want to measure as part of a survey. Constructs can be relatively easy to define or measure, such as the number of times someone does exercise per week, or something more abstract, such as confidence.

Convenience sample a type of non-probability sample. A convenience sample is one that is drawn from a group of people or other sampling units that are 'to hand', sampling whoever is convenient to the researcher.

Correlation where changes in one variable are related to changes in another variable, but we do not know whether change in one variable consistently causes change in another – the variables are simply related. This is in contrast to causation.

Coverage error a type of error that occurs when the sampling frame isn't matched perfectly to the target population. Some groups of people are missing from the sampling frame or some groups overrepresented.

Cross-sectional study cross-sectional studies gather data at a particular point in time, giving a 'snapshot' of what is happening at that moment.

Dependent interviewing an interviewing strategy unique to longitudinal studies aimed at reducing measurement error. Dependent interviewing uses information already known about the respondent to personalise the questions they receive at later waves of a study.

Experimental data where researchers control what participants are exposed to by manipulating events or situations and then see how outcomes differ depending on what has been manipulated.

External validity in the context of a longitudinal study, and sampling in particular, external validity is where inferences can be made from the sample to the population as a whole – in other words, the sample accurately represents the population.

Hawthorne effect the phenomenon where the act of observing or measuring something changes the thing that is being measured, if the subject of interest is aware that they are being observed or measured.

Heterogeneous something that is heterogeneous means that multiple items or units are different from one another. In the context of a longitudinal study, we often use the term 'heterogeneous' in relation to a sample to describe when sample members are different from one another. Heterogeneous is in contrast to homogeneous.

Homogeneous something that is homogeneous means that multiple items or units are the same or similar in some way. In the context of a longitudinal study, we often use the term 'homogeneous' in relation to a sample to describe when sample members are the same or similar to one another. Homogeneous is in contrast to heterogenous.

Imputation a method for dealing with missing data. Imputation is the process of replacing missing values with estimated ones. The estimations can be based on information known about the respondent already, from information known about the population of interest or from information from another case that shares similarities to the respondent with missing values.

Item non-response a type of missingness. In the context of a survey, item non-response is where somebody participates in the survey but doesn't answer all the questions, resulting in gaps in the dataset.

Longitudinal study a study that follows the same sampling units of time, taking repeated measurements at multiple time intervals. A longitudinal study allows change or stability over time within individuals to be observed.

Measurement error a type of error that occurs in the measurement stage of data collection, where there is a difference between the measured value of something and the true value.

Missing at Random a type of missing data. Missing at Random (MAR) is where the propensity for data to be missing has nothing to do with the variable or measurement of interest, but the missingness is systematically related to a different observed variable. This is in contract to Missing Completely at Random (MCAR) and Missing not at Random (MNAR).

Missing Completely at Random a type of missing data. Missing Completely at Random (MCAR) is where there is no difference between missing data and observed data (or at least for data which the researcher has access to) – that is to say, the missingness of the data hasn't caused any bias. This is in contract to Missing at Random (MAR) and Missing not at Random (MNAR).

Missing not at Random a type of missing data. Missing not at Random (MNAR) is where the value of the variable that is missing is related in some way to the reason why it is missing. This is in contract to Missing at Random (MAR) and Missing Completely at Random (MCAR).

Mode effects the effect the mode of interviewing might have had on the responses given to different questions by different people. Mode effects can introduce systematic bias into data.

Modes the method by which data is collected. For example, the mode could be face-to-face, telephone or online.

Monotone missing a missing data pattern found in longitudinal data. Monotone missing data means that there is continuous data available for an individual for multiple waves of a longitudinal study up to a certain point and then no more data is available. This happens when a respondent drops out of a longitudinal study at a certain point and is then never interviewed again. This is in contrast to non-monotone missing.

Natural experiment an experiment not where researchers have manipulated events or conditions for certain groups of people in the traditional sense of an experiment, but where manipulation has occurred naturally in the real world. Different people end up in different conditions or circumstances as a result of something external that has happened.

Non-differentiation a problem that occurs when respondents fail to read and respond to each specific question, and rather provide the same answer for every question rather than the true or accurate answer. It is particularly likely to occur when grids of questions are used. Non-differentiation is also known as 'straightlining'. The impact of non-differentiation is the introduction of measurement error into data.

Non-monotone missing a missing data pattern found in longitudinal data. Non-monotone missing data means that data are available for an individual only for certain waves of a longitudinal study; there are gaps in the data. This happens when a respondent does not participate in a longitudinal study at certain waves, but is interviewed at some point subsequently. This is in contrast to monotone missing.

Non-probability sample a sample where non-random methods are used to select a sample, utilising more subjective methods instead. Research conducted on data collected from a non-probability sample means that it is difficult to assess how well results from the research can be inferred to the population of interest as a whole. A non-probability sample is in contrast to a probability sample.

Non-response bias a type of bias introduced when those who choose not to participate in a study are systematically different in some way from those who do take part. This can result in the sample not representing the population as a whole.

Observational study an observational study is one where researchers observe what is happening, but they do not manipulate or influence events. Observational data can be collected using interviews or questionnaires by the researcher watching and noting situations or behaviours, or by administrative information about individuals being used.

Panel conditioning a phenomenon unique to longitudinal studies, where an individual's response to a question at a particular point in time is influenced by a response they gave at a previous time point or, more broadly, by simply the fact that they are involved in a longitudinal study.

Participant burden the degree to which a respondent feels that participating in a survey has been time-consuming, difficult or emotionally challenging. Burden can lead to participants either giving data of lower quality because it is difficult to provide accurate data or not participating at all.

Period effects effects that affect everybody, of any age, at the same time. These are usually external things, such as economic depression or civil unrest. Period effects are in contrast to age effects and cohort effects.

Population in the context of a longitudinal study, the population is the entire group that the study is interested in. For example, this could be all the people who live in a particular country, or all the people who attend a certain school or work in a particular sector.

Primacy effects the phenomenon whereby in visual modes of survey administration, such as paper or online, if respondents are presented with a long list of response options, they are more likely to select options towards the top of the list. Primacy effects can introduce measurement error into data.

Priming in the context of a survey, priming refers to the phenomenon where exposure to one particular topic or issue in a survey can then influence responses to questions later in the survey.

Probability sample a sample where the probability of any individual sampling unit being included in the sample is known in advance. The probability of inclusion does not have to be equal for all sampling units, but it has to be known. A probability sampling method is likely to be representative of the population of interest. A probability sample is in contrast to a non-probability sample.

Prospective longitudinal studies in the context of longitudinal studies, prospective studies is where individuals are recruited and then followed over time to assess outcomes. The group followed are often representative of a general population, and the study aims to understand factors that contribute to different outcomes.

Questionnaire routing in a survey, the tailoring of follow-up questions based on responses to previous questions.

Quota sample a type of non-probability sample. A quota sample is where the researcher first thinks about the types of people they want to include in their sample, then sets up targets for the numbers or proportions of people with different characteristics who should be included in the sample.

Recency effects the phenomenon whereby in audio modes of survey administration, such as telephone, if respondents are presented with a long list of response options, they are more likely to select options towards the end of the list. Recency effects can introduce measurement error into data.

Refresh the sample refreshing the sample is where new sample members are added to a study once it is underway; it is utilised almost exclusively in longitudinal research. This is usually done to counter the fact that people drop out of longitudinal studies. To ensure that the sample remains representative of the population of interest, a refreshment sample is added, consisting of people who fit the original study eligibility criteria.

Repeated cross-sectional studies if a cross-sectional design is one where data is gathered data at a particular point in time to give a snapshot of what is happening, a repeated cross-sectional design is where snapshots are gathered at multiple points in time. This allows change and stability over time to be assessed at the population level, but it does not allow an assessment of individual level change over time.

Representative in the context of longitudinal studies and sampling, representativeness means that the sample chosen to represent the population of interest does so accurately. This in turn means that research findings from the study can be applied to the population of interest confidently.

Retrospective longitudinal studies these follow the same people across a period of time, but often participants must have already experienced an outcome of interest in order to be part of the study. Information is then collected about events from the past in order to understand outcomes.

Sample the group of units (people, households, businesses, and so on) that belong to the population that is under study and aim to represent that population of interest accurately.

Sampling error a type of error that occurs in statistical analysis when the sampling units do not represent the population of interest. This means that bias is introduced into the data and resultant analysis, resulting in the statistical results not being completely applicable to the population of interest.

Sampling frame a sampling frame is a list, or register, of all the members of the population of interest. From this list, a representative sample can be drawn for a longitudinal study.

Sampling unit the entities that are chosen to represent the population of interest in a longitudinal study and followed over time as part of the study. In a longitudinal study, sampling units are most often people or households.

Satisficing a strategy whereby respondents use short-cuts in order to provide a response that they think will appear to be acceptable, rather than providing an optimal response. Satisficing behaviour may be more prevalent when the task at hand is cognitively challenging or burdensome to a respondent. Satisficing can introduce measurement error into data.

Seam bias a problem unique to longitudinal studies, where estimates of change across the 'seam' (between two waves of a longitudinal study) are far greater than estimates of change that are measured within the reference period of a single survey ('within waves'); specifically, too many changes are seen at the seam and too few within a wave. Seam bias is a form of measurement error.

Secondary data sources data that has already been collected by someone else, as opposed to a researcher directly collecting their own source data (through surveys or interviews, for example).

Selection bias a type of bias where groups of individuals in one condition are systematically different in some way from groups of individuals in another condition, meaning a comparison of the two groups cannot be done robustly. In the context of surveys, selection bias may be introduced when certain types of people are more likely to choose or be able to use different modes of completion. This can result in the sample not representing the population as a whole.

Simple random sample a type of probability sample. A simple random sample is a sampling method by which each of the sampling units have an equal chance of being chosen through being chosen completely at random. A simple random sample, if it is large enough, should give a sample which is representative of the population from which it was drawn. This means that any findings of research conducted on members of that sample should be unbiased (notwithstanding the introduction of other errors) and therefore generalisable to the population as a whole.

Snowball sample a type of non-probability sample. A snowball sample is where a researcher finds a few people with certain characteristics that they are interested in, including in their sample. They then ask these respondents if they know of other people who also fit the group of interest, generating more sample members in this way. This is a good technique for capturing minority population groups or people who wouldn't usually participate in research. Snowball sampling is also known as respondent-driving sampling.

Social desirability bias where a survey respondent fails to answer a question accurately if they believe their answer is not a socially desirable thing to say. Rather than give the embarrassing or undesirable answer, they give an answer that they believe is socially desirable or acceptable. Social desirability bias introduces measurement error into data.

Straightlining see 'non-differentiation'.

Strata when a stratified sampling method is used, the population of interest is divided into homogeneous groups. Each of those groups is called a strata.

Stratified sample a type of probability sample. A stratified sample is where the population of interest is divided into different groups and then individuals within those groups are chosen to form part of the sample. The initial groups are chosen based on common characteristics, which means the resultant sample contains representatives from each of those groups. Each group is referred to as a strata.

Sweep see 'wave'.

Target population the group of people, or population, that a study intends to represent.

Telescoping in the context of a longitudinal study, telescoping is a type of recall problem where respondents can perceive recent events as happening longer ago than they actually did (backward telescoping), and events from a long time ago happening more recently than they did (forward telescoping).

Tracing in the context of a longitudinal study, tracing is the act of locating, or tracking, study members over time. Often, individuals or households move address or change contact details, and so the study has to locate or trace them at each wave in order to invite them to participate.

Unbalanced panel where in a longitudinal dataset, some measurements are missing for some sampling units at some waves – in other words, the dataset contains missing data. This is in contrast to a balanced panel.

Unit non-response A type of missingness. In the context of a survey, unit non-response is where somebody doesn't participate in the survey, resulting in data for them – the unit – being missing from the dataset.

Wave in a longitudinal study, a wave is a follow-up point, so each wave could be each time a follow-up survey is conducted. The baseline survey is the first wave of data collection. Sometimes the word 'sweep' is used instead of wave.

Weighting a method for dealing with missing data. Weighting gives different 'importance' to certain underrepresented groups in a survey, meaning that analysis conducted using weights is more applicable to the population of interest than analysis of the same data without using weights.

References

American Association for Public Opinion Research (2022) Standard definitions. Available at: www.aapor.org/Standards-Ethics/Standard-Definitions-(1).aspx (accessed 10 April 2023).

Ansolabehere, S. and Schaffner, B.F. (2015) 'Distractions: The incidence and consequences of interruptions for survey respondents', *Journal of Survey Statistics and Methodology*, 3 (2): 216–39.

Axinn, W.G., Gatny, H.H. and Wagner, J. (2015) 'Maximizing data quality using mode switching in mixed-device survey design: Nonresponse bias and models of demographic behavior', *Methoden Daten Analysen*, 9 (2): 163–84.

Baek, S. and Choi, E.-H. (2021) 'A longitudinal analysis of alcohol use behavior among Korean adults and related factors: A latent class growth model', *International Journal of Environmental Research and Public Health*, 18 (16): 8797.

Basic, E. and Rendtel, U. (2007) 'Assessing the bias due to non-coverage of residential movers in the German Microcensus Panel: An evaluation using data from the Socio-Economic Panel', *AStA Advances in Statistical Analysis*, 91 (3): 311–34.

Beckett, M., DaVanzo, J., Sastry, N., Panis, C. and Peterson, C. (2001) 'The quality of retrospective data: An examination of long-term recall in a developing country', *Journal of Human Resources*, 36 (3): 593–625.

Berrington, A. and Diamond, I. (2000) 'Marriage or cohabitation: A competing risks analysis of first-partnership formation among the 1958 British birth cohort', *Journal of the Royal Statistical Society*. Series A (Statistics in Society), 163 (2): 127–51.

Bianchi, A., Biffignandi, S. and Lynn, P. (2017) 'Web-face-to-face mixed-mode design in a longitudinal survey: Effects on participation rates, sample composition, and costs', *Journal of Official Statistics*, 33 (2): 385–408.

Blanchard, R.D., Bunker, J.B. and Wachs, M. (1977) 'Distinguishing aging, period and cohort effects in longitudinal studies of elderly populations', *Socio-Economic Planning Sciences*, 11 (3): 137–46.

Bowling, A. and Windsor, J. (2008) 'The effects of question order and response-choice on self-rated health status in the English Longitudinal Study of Ageing (ELSA)', *Journal of Epidemiology & Community Health*, 62 (1): 81–5.

Brown, N.R., Rips, L.J. and Shevell, S.K. (1985) 'The subjective dates of natural events in very-long-term memory', *Cognitive Psychology*, 17 (2): 139–77.

Bruin-Huisman, L., Abu-Hanna, A., Henk, C.P.M., van Weert, H.C.P.M. and Beers, E. (2017) 'Potentially inappropriate prescribing to older patients in primary care in the Netherlands: A retrospective longitudinal study', *Age and Ageing*, 46 (4): 614–19.

Cepeda, A. and Valdez, A. (2010) 'Ethnographic strategies in the tracking and retention of street-recruited community-based samples of substance using hidden populations in longitudinal studies', *Substance Use & Misuse*, 45 (5): 700–16.

Chan, D. (1998) 'The conceptualization and analysis of change over time: An integrative approach incorporating longitudinal mean and covariance structures analysis (LMACS) and multiple indicator latent growth modeling (MLGM)', *Organizational Research Methods*, 1 (4): 421–83.

Collishaw, S., Maughan, B., Natarajan, L. and Pickles, A. (2010) 'Trends in adolescent emotional problems in England: A comparison of two national cohorts twenty years apart', *Journal of Child Psychology and Psychiatry*, 51 (8): 885–94.

Conrad, F.G., Couper, M.P., Tourangeau, R. and Zhang, C. (2017) 'Reducing speeding in web surveys by providing immediate feedback', *Survey Research Methods*, 11 (1): 45–61.

Couper, M.P., Singer, E. and Tourangeau, R. (2003) 'Understanding the effects of audio-casi on self-reports of sensitive behavior', *Public Opinion Quarterly*, 67 (3): 385–95.

Davis, M.M., McGonagle, K., Schoeni, R.F. and Stafford, F. (2015) 'Grandparental and parental obesity influences on childhood overweight: Implications for primary care practice', *Journal of the American Board of Family Medicine*, 21 (6): 549–54.

Dillman, D., Phelps, G., Tortora, R., Swift, K., Kohrell, J., Berck, J. and Messer, B.L. (2009) 'Response rate and measurement differences in mixed-mode surveys using mail, telephone, interactive voice response (IVR) and the Internet', *Social Science Research*, 38 (1): 1–18.

Fisher, P. (2019) 'Does repeated measurement improve income data quality?', *Oxford Bulletin of Economics and Statistics*, 81 (5): 989–1011.

Frick, J.R. and Grabka, M.M. (2010) 'Item nonresponse and imputation of annual labor income in panel surveys from a cross national perspective', in Harkness, J.A., Braun, M., Edwards, B., Johnson, T.P., Lyberg, L.E., Mohler, P. Pennell, B. and Smith, T.W. (eds) *Survey Methods in Multinational, Multiregional, and Multicultural Contexts*. Hoboken, NJ: John Wiley & Son.

Goodman, A., Brown, M., Silverwood, R.J., Sakshaug, J.W., Calderwood, L., Williams, J. and Ploubidis, G.B. (2022) 'The impact of using the Web in a mixed-mode follow-up of a longitudinal birth cohort study: Evidence from the National Child Development Study', *Journal of the Royal Statistical Society*. Series A (Statistics in Society), 185 (3): 822–50.

Halpern-Manners, A., Warren, J.R. and Torche, F. (2017) 'Panel conditioning in the general social survey', *Sociological Methods & Research*, 46 (1): 103–24.

Hammond, F., McNeill, B. and Cummings, K.M. (2006) 'Effectiveness of cigarette warning labels in informing smokers about the risks of smoking: Findings from the International Tobacco Control (ITC) four country survey', *PubMed Central*, 15 (3): 19–25.

Harling, G., Perkins, J.M., Gómez-Olivé, F.X., Morris, K., Wagner, R.G., Montana, L., Kabudula, C.W., Bärnighausen, T., Kahn, K. and Berkman, L. (2018) 'Interviewer-driven variability in social network reporting: Results from Health and Aging in Africa: A longitudinal study of an INDEPTH community (HAALSI) in South Africa', *Field Methods*, 30 (2): 140–54.

Heerwegh, D. (2009) 'Mode differences between face-to-face and web surveys: An experimental investigation of data quality and social desirability effects', *International Journal of Public Opinion Research*, 21 (1): 111–21.

Heerwegh, D. and Loosveldt, G. (2008) 'Face-to-face versus web surveying in a high-internet-coverage population: Differences in response quality', *Public Opinion Quarterly*, 72 (5): 836–46.

Hohl, K., Stanko, B. and Newburn, T. (2012) 'The effect of the 2011 London disorder on public opinion of police and attitudes towards crime, disorder, and sentencing', *Policing: A Journal of Policy and Practice*, 7 (1): 12–20.

Hox, J.J. and de Leeuw, E.D. (1994) 'A comparison of nonresponse in mail, telephone, and face-to-face surveys: Applying multilevel modeling to meta-analysis', *Quality & Quantity*, 28 (1): 329–44.

Jarvis, S. and Jenkins, S.P. (1996) 'Changing places: Income mobility and poverty dynamics in Britain', Working paper 96–16, ESRC Research Centre on Micro-Social Change. Colchester: University of Essex.

Javanbakht, M., Lin, J., Ragsdale, A., Kim, S., Siminski, S. and Gorbach, F. (2022) 'Comparing single and multiple imputation strategies for harmonizing substance use data across HIV-related cohort studies', *BMC Medical Research Methodology*, 22 (90).

Johns, R. (2005) 'One size doesn't fit all: Selecting response scales for attitude items', *Journal of Elections, Public Opinion and Parties*, 15 (2): 237–64.

Kemp, S. (1999) 'An associative theory of estimating past dates and past prices', *Psychonomic Bulletin & Review*, 6 (1): 41–56.

Kraut, R.E. and McConahay, J.B. (1973) 'How being interviewed affects voting: An experiment', *Public Opinion Quarterly*, 37 (3): 398–406.

Krosnick, J.A. (1991) 'Response strategies for coping with the cognitive demands of attitude measures in survey', *Applied Cognitive Psychology*, 5 (3): 213–36.

Krosnick, J.A. and Alwin, D.F. (1987) 'An evaluation of a cognitive theory of response order effects in survey measurement', *Public Opinion Quarterly*, 51 (2): 201–19.

Kühne, S. (2018) 'From strangers to acquaintances? Interviewer continuity and socially desirable responses in panel surveys', *Survey Research Methods*, 12 (2): 121–46.

Lavrakas, P.J. (2008) 'Respondent burden', in Lavrakas, P.J. (ed.) *Encyclopedia of Survey Research Methods*. Thousand Oaks, CA: Sage Publications.

Lee, H.Y., Kim, M.S., Kim, O., Lee, I.H. and Kim, H.K. (2016) 'Association between shift work and severity of depressive symptoms among female nurses: The Korea Nurses' Health Study', *Journal of Nursing Management*, 24 (2): 192–200.

Li, Y.I., Starr, L.R. and Wray-Lake, L. (2018) 'Insomnia mediates the longitudinal relationship between anxiety and depressive symptoms in a nationally representative sample of adolescents', *Depression and Anxiety*, 35 (6): 583–91.

Maitland, A. (2009) 'Should I label all scale points or just the end points for attitudinal questions?', *Survey Practice*, 2 (4).

Malhotra, N. (2008) 'Completion time and response order effects in web surveys', *Public Opinion Quarterly*, 72 (5): 914–34.

Menard, S. (2007) *Handbook of Longitudinal Research*. New York: Academic Press.

Moore, J., Bates, N., Pascale, J. and Okon, A. (2009) 'Tackling seam bias through questionnaire design', in Lynn, P. (ed.) *Methodology of Longitudinal Surveys*. Chichester: John Wiley & Sons.

Morton, S.M.B., Atatoa Carr, P.E., Bandara, D.K., Grant, C.C., Ivory, V.C., Kingi, T.R., Liang, R., Perese, L.M., Peterson, E., Pryor, J.E., Reese, E., Robinson, E.M., Schmidt, J.M., and Waldie, K.E. (2010) 'Growing up in New Zealand: A longitudinal study of New Zealand children and their families. Report 1: Before we are born'. Auckland: *Growing up in New Zealand*.

Osmond, C., Barker, D.J.P., Winter, P.D., Fall, C.H.D and Simmonds, S.J. (1993) 'Early growth and death from cardiovascular disease in women', *British Medical Journal*, 307 (6918): 1519–24.

Plewis, I. (ed.) (2007) *The Millennium Cohort Study: Technical Report on Sampling* (4th edn). London: Centre for Longitudinal Studies.

Ployhart, R.E. and Vandenberg, R.J. (2010) 'Longitudinal research: The theory, design, and analysis of change', *Journal of Management*, 36 (1): 94–120.

Rips, L.J., Conrad, F.G. and Fricker, S.S. (2003) 'Straightening the seam effect in panel surveys', *Public Opinion Quarterly*, 67 (4): 522–54.

Rubin, D.C. and Baddeley, A.D. (1989) 'Telescoping is not time compression: A model of the dating of autobiographical event', *Memory & Cognition*, 17 (6): 653–61.

Schoon, I., Ross, A. and Martin, P. (2009) 'Sequences, patterns, and variations in the assumption of work and family-related roles: Evidence from two British birth cohorts', in Schoon, I. and Silbereisen, R.K. (eds) *Transitions from School to Work: Globalisation, Individualisation, and Patterns of Diversity*. Cambridge: Cambridge University Press, pp. 219–42.

Singer, J.D. and Willett, J.B. (2003) *Applied Longitudinal Data Analysis*. New York: Oxford University Press.

Smith, T.W. (1984) 'A preliminary analysis of methodological experiments on the 1984 GSS', GSS Technical Report No. 49. Chicago: NORC.

Toepoel, V. and Lugtig, P. (2022) 'Modularization in an era of mobile web: Investigating the effects of cutting a survey into smaller pieces on data quality', *Social Science Computer Review*, 40 (1): 150–64.

Tooth, L., Ware, R., Bain, C., Purdie, D.M. and Dobson, A. (2005) 'Quality of reporting of observational longitudinal research', *Practice of Epidemiology*, 161 (3): 280–8.

Tourangeau, R., Steiger, D.M. and Wilson, D. (2002) 'Self-administered questions by telephone: Evaluating interactive voice response', *Public Opinion Quarterly*, 66 (2): 265–78.

Turkson, A.J., Ayiah-Mensah, F. and Nimoh, V. (2021) 'Handling censoring and censored data in survival analysis: A standalone systematic literature review', *International Journal of Mathematics and Mathematical Sciences*, 2021.

Tzavidis, N., Salvati, N., Schmid, T., Flouri, E. and Midouhas, E. (2016) 'Longitudinal analysis of the strengths and difficulties questionnaire scores of the Millennium Cohort Study children in England using M-quantile random-effects regression', *Journal of the Royal Statistical Society*. Series A (Statistics in Society), 179 (2): 427–52.

Understanding Society User Guide (last revised 29 October 2020). Colchester: Institute for Social and Economic Research.

Wang, M., Beal, D.J., Chan, D., Newman, D.A., Vancouver, J.B. and Vandenberg, R.J. (2017) 'Longitudinal research: A panel discussion on conceptual issues, research design, and statistical techniques', *Work, Aging and Retirement*, 3 (1): 1–24.

Warren, J.R. and Halpern-Manners, A. (2012) 'Panel conditioning in longitudinal social science surveys', *Sociological Methods & Research*, 41 (4): 491–534.

Yan, T., Keusch, F. and He, L. (2018) 'The impact of question and scale characteristics on scale direction effects', *Survey Practice*, 11 (2).

Young, A.F., Powers, J.R. and Bell, S.L. (2006) 'Attrition in longitudinal studies: Who do you lose?', *Australian and New Zealand Journal of Public Health*, 30 (4): 353–61.

Zwane, A.P., Zinman, J., Van Dusen, E., Pariente, W., Null, C., Miguel, E., Kremer, M., Karlan, D.S., Hornbeck, R., Giné, X., Duflo, E., Devoto, F., Crepon, B. and Banerjee, A. (2011) 'Being surveyed can change later behavior and related parameter estimates', *Proceedings of the National Academy of Sciences*, 108 (5): 1821–6.

Index